Sexual Harassment

Recent Titles in
Bibliographies and Indexes in Women's Studies

Women and Mass Communications: An International Annotated Bibliography
John A. Lent

Sources on the History of Women's Magazines, 1792–1960: An Annotated Bibliography
Mary Ellen Zuckerman, compiler

Feminist Research Methods: An Annotated Bibliography
Connie Miller with Corinna Treitel

War and Peace through Women's Eyes: A Selective Bibliography of Twentieth-Century American Women's Fiction
Susanne Carter

American Women Playwrights, 1900–1930: A Checklist
Frances Diodato Bzowski, compiler

Women in Japanese Society: An Annotated Bibliography of Selected English Language Materials
Kristina Ruth Huber, with Kathryn Sparling

United States Government Documents on Women, 1800–1990: A Comprehensive Bibliography, Volume I: Social Issues
Mary Ellen Huls

United States Government Documents on Women, 1800–1990: A Comprehensive Bibliography, Volume II: Labor
Mary Ellen Huls

Mothers and Daughters in American Short Fiction: An Annotated Bibliography of Twentieth-Century Women's Literature
Susanne Carter, compiler

Women and Work in Developing Countries: An Annotated Bibliography
Parvin Ghorayshi, compiler

Acquaintance and Date Rape: An Annotated Bibliography
Sally K. Ward, Jennifer Dziuba-Leatherman, Jane Gerard Stapleton, and Carrie L. Yodanis, compilers

French Women Playwrights before the Twentieth Century: A Checklist
Cecilia Beach, compiler

Sexual Harassment

A Selected, Annotated Bibliography

Lynda Jones Hartel
and Helena M. VonVille

Bibliographies and Indexes in Women's Studies, *Number 23*

Greenwood Press
Westport, Connecticut • London

Library of Congress Cataloging-in-Publication Data

Hartel, Lynda Jones.
    Sexual harassment : a selected, annotated bibliography / Lynda
Jones Hartel and Helena M. VonVille.
        p.   cm.—(Bibliographies and indexes in women's studies,
    ISSN 0742-6941 ; no. 23)
    Includes indexes.
    ISBN 0-313-29055-5 (alk. paper)
    1. Sexual harassment of women—United States—Bibliography.
2. Sexual harassment of women—Law and legislation—United States—
Bibliography.   3. Sexual harassment—United States—Bibliography.
4. Sexual harassment—Law and legislation—Unired States—
Bibliography.   I. VonVille, Helena M.   II. Title.   III. Series.
Z7164.S46H37   1995
[HQ1237.5.U6]
016.30542—dc20   95-21267

British Library Cataloguing in Publication Data is available.

Library of Congress Catalog Card Number: 95-21267
ISBN: 0-313-29055-5
ISSN: 0742-6941

First published in 1995

Greenwood Press, 88 Post Road West, Westport, CT 06881
An imprint of Greenwood Publishing Group, Inc.

Printed in the United States of America

The paper used in this book complies with the
Permanent Paper Standard issued by the National
Information Standards Organization (Z39.48–1984).

10 9 8 7 6 5 4 3 2

Contents

Preface

In 1985, M. Dawn McCaghy published *Sexual Harassment: A Guide to Resources*, an annotated bibliography covering the sexual harassment literature from 1974-1984. In the intervening years, we have seen an explosion of interest and, subsequently, articles and books on the topic. This work picks up where McCaghy left off and continues through 1994.

This volume, the result of nearly three years of intense research and study, was born of both personal experience and the authors' conviction that sexual harassment is an important, albeit confusing, issue facing all of us. We cannot consider it "just" a woman's issue; it is a human issue. Consequently, it is our hope that this publication will serve as a useful resource for all those who study this sensitive area.

Without a great deal of assistance, a work of this nature could not be completed. The authors wish to thank the staff of the John A. Prior Health Sciences Library, The Ohio State University. A special debt of gratitude goes to Judy Willis and her interlibrary loan staff for their always-present willingness to track down books and journals, and to Claire Kitchen and her document delivery staff for assistance with the seemingly never-ending task of photocopying. Thanks also go to Melanie Putnam of The Ohio State University Law Library for assisting with the legal research involved in this project. And special thanks go to the staff at the Education/Psychology Library, The Ohio State University, for their support, assistance, and advice. This work was supported in part by a grant from the Academic Committee on Research, University Libraries, The Ohio State University.

We are grateful, too, for the support of our friends and family members. Special appreciation goes to Ms. Hartel's husband, Jeff, for his enduring patience, practical advice, and encouragement during the research and writing of this book, and to Kimberly Weber for her many hours of labor in keeping the authors organized.

Introduction

The problem of sexual harassment was with us long before the highly publicized 1991 confirmation hearings for Supreme Court Justice Clarence Thomas. However, Anita Hill's testimony regarding sexual harassment captured the nation and sparked a public debate on what had been treated as a very private issue.

At first glance the issue of sexual harassment may seem simple but the definitions of sexual harassment actually cover a wide range of behaviors. From subtle innuendoes or jokes to explicit demands for sexual relations in exchange for career opportunities, sexual harassment is both pervasive and perplexing. What is harassment to one is in poor taste to another and may be perfectly acceptable to another. Because of the very subjective nature of sexual harassment, it is difficult to quantify and define.

It is because of the pervasiveness and complexity of sexual harassment that there now exists an enormous body of literature on this topic. Although an initial search yielded over a thousand citations concerning sexual harassment, we have included 535 references here. The many articles, books, and dissertations included in this bibliography were selected on the basis of their scholarly, original, or creative contribution to sexual harassment literature. This resource guide is designed for students, researchers, librarians, legal professionals, and personnel officers.

Print materials published between January 1984 and late 1994 which deal with sexual harassment in the United States are contained in this bibliography. Materials generally omitted were: editorial comments or letters; generic works on harassment; materials not readily available in the United States; newspaper articles; popular press publications; materials whose primary focus was on rape, sexual abuse, incest, or racial discrimination; anecdotal reports; and articles specific to the Packwood or Tail Hook controversies. Articles on the Thomas-Hill hearings were selectively included.

Bibliographic references were drawn from: *Books in Print, Business Periodicals Index, Cumulative Index to Nursing and Allied Health Literature (CINAHL), Dissertation Abstracts International, Educational Resources*

Information Center (ERIC), FirstSearch, Legal Resources Index, LegalTrac, MEDLINE, PsycLIT, Social Sciences Index, SocioFile, and citations in works examined.

Except for the doctoral dissertations, each item has been personally examined and annotated. Annotations are descriptive in nature, not evaluative, and attempt to note special features of the material, such as sample sexual harassment policies and grievance forms. When possible, the number of materials cited by authors are noted (exceptions to this are legal materials and most books). Acronyms or abbreviations used include:

SH = sexual harassment
EEOC = Equal Employment Opportunity Commission
Civil Rights Act = 1964 Civil Rights Act
Title VII = Title VII of the 1964 Civil Rights Act
Title IX = Title IX of the Education Amendments of 1972

Entries are organized in four (4) main parts and eighteen (18) chapters. Part 1 examines the history, theories, and consequences of sexual harassment. Part 2 addresses sexual harassment in various workplace settings. Part 3 discusses sexual harassment in academic, social, and living environments. Part 4 explores the legal aspects of sexual harassment.

Entries fitting into two or more chapters are placed in the most logical chapter, with additional access provided by the subject index. Index terms are based on the Library of Congress Subject Headings (15th ed., 1992), with adaptations made as necessary.

For the readers' convenience, a brief chronology of significant sexual harassment legislation and publications is appended. The subject and author indices follow this appendix.

Sexual Harassment

1

The Nature of Sexual Harassment: History, Theory, and Research

1. Bingham, Shereen G., ed. *Conceptualizing Sexual Harassment as Discursive Practice*. Westport, CT: Praeger, 1994.

    This series of articles explores what is known about SH, how it has been studied, and possible new directions to pursue. Bingham and a variety of contributing authors discuss such issues as gender socialization, power, and communication. Some of these articles had originally appeared in the *Journal of Applied Communication Research.*

2. Davidson, Nicholas. "Feminism and sexual harassment." *Society* 28:4 (May/June 1991), 39-44.

    Davidson discusses the feminist perspective of SH, which he asserts offers much to be denied. The author believes that regulations designed to control sexually harassing behaviors will not provide the benefits expected, and that a more "natural" approach, one which allows for a certain degree of tension between men and women, should be allowed to exist. Unisexism, female chauvinism, and oppression are examined.

3. Dodds, Susan M., Lucy Frost, Robert Pargetter, and Elizabeth W. Prior. "Sexual harassment." *Social Theory and Practice* 14:2 (Summer 1988), 111-130.

    The authors argue for a behavioral stipulative definition of SH, asserting that it is more useful for policy purposes than ordinary language concepts. They define and examine the differences between SH, harassment, and legitimate sexual interactions.

4.   Fitzgerald, Louise F., and Sandra L. Shullman. "Sexual harassment: A research analysis and agenda for the 1990s." *Journal of Vocational Behavior* 42:1 (February 1993), 5-27.

      An overview of SH research of women in the workplace is provided. Incidence and prevalence studies as well as perceptions and attributions are presented as major research areas to date, and two emerging areas of study are identified: victim response and coping behaviors, and workplace factors. The authors suggest that an examination of workplace factors can lead to better intervention. A research agenda is offered. (81 refs).

5.   "Gender, race and the politics of Supreme Court appointments: The import of the Anita Hill/Clarence Thomas hearings." *Southern California Law Review* 65:3 (March 1992), 1279-1582.

      Over twenty essays, articles, and speeches concerning the myths, nature, and law of SH are assembled in this special volume. Published only six months after the Thomas-Hill hearings, the entries reflect the intense national interest in SH generated by Anita Hill's allegations against Clarence Thomas.

6.   Gillespie, Dair L., and Ann Leffler. "The politics of research methodology in claims-making activities: Social science and sexual harassment." *Social Problems* 34:5 (December 1987), 490-501.

      The authors use SH research as a case study of scientific claims-making activity. As emergent social problems become politicized, a bias results which is reflected in the theories that are developed, the research methodologies used, and the analysis and reporting of the results. They conclude that methodological as well as theoretical questions must be considered when examining the evolution of social problems. (60 refs).

7.   Gruber, James E. "How women handle sexual harassment: A literature review." *Sociology and Social Research* 74:1 (October 1989), 3-9.

      In a review of the literature, the author discusses two primary difficulties involved in comparing the results of SH studies. First, each researcher seems to have developed unique categories of SH response types. Second, researchers have paid too little attention to variations in wording or content of the categories. To remedy this, the author extracts from the existing research literature an exhaustive categorization of responses to SH. Using his typology, he is able to organize and classify research done in the area. (23 refs).

8. Gruber, James E. "Methodological problems and policy implications in sexual harassment research." *Population Research and Policy Review* 9:3 (September 1990), 235-254.

    Gruber focuses on several methodological problems and unanswered questions in the existing SH literature. An analysis of the empirical research literature to define SH, he feels, will facilitate the comparison of research results, legal arguments, and policy decision making in the workplace. Research on perception of SH can be used, according to the author, to create a standard of harassment severity. Recommendations are offered for areas of future research. (50 refs).

9. Gruber, James E. "A typology of personal and environmental sexual harassment: Research and policy implications for the 1990s." *Sex Roles* 26:11/12 (June 1992), 447-464.

    The author describes a systematic categorization of sexual harassment which reflects the 1988 guidelines of the Equal Employment Opportunity Commission (EEOC). In analyzing 17 studies and evaluating the sexual harassment categories, two critical issues were discovered: 1) the lack of a coherent and consistent vocabulary within the studies; and 2) the categories were not mutually exclusive or exhaustive. The author distinguishes between 11 categories of SH (4 types of verbal requests, 3 verbal remarks, and 4 nonverbal displays) with each category having one or more types of behaviors consistent with the EEOC guidelines. (49 refs).

10. Kreps, Gary L., ed. *Sexual Harassment: Communication Implications.* Cresskill, NJ: Hampton Press, Inc., 1993.

    This book focuses on the role of communication in SH and communicative strategies for managing SH in the workplace. From organizational romance to SH in the movies, SH on the college campus to cultural adaptation, this volume represents a broad range of approaches for preventing SH through communication.

11. Lach, Denise H., and Patricia A. Gwartney-Gibbs. "Sociological perspectives on sexual harassment and workplace dispute resolution." *Journal of Vocational Behavior* 42:1 (February 1993), 102-115.

    The authors present a theoretical framework which suggests that SH disputes are a visible example of workplace disputes that consistently disadvantage women. The framework describes disputes as consisting of origins, processes, and outcomes patterned by an individual's sex, race, and occupation. Empirical research on SH is examined within this framework. (56 refs).

12. Lebacqz, Karen. "Justice and sexual harassment." *Capital University Law Review* 22 (Summer 1993), 605-622.

     Focusing on SH as a violation of justice, the author suggests that hostile environment SH requires attention to the paradigm of injustice as oppression. Oppression, she believes, is levied against individuals as members of groups, is socially structured, and is built into cultural myths and stereotypes.

13. McCaghy, M. Dawn. *Sexual Harassment: A Guide to Resources.* Boston: G. K. Hall & Co., 1985.

     This annotated bibliography on SH cites 299 popular press and scholarly books, reports, periodical articles, and training materials published between 1974 and 1984. The majority of McCaghy's entries deal with SH in U.S. academic and business settings. Author, title, and subject indices are included.

14. Minson, J. P. "Social theory and legal argument: Catharine MacKinnon on sexual harassment." *International Journal of the Sociology of Law* 19:3 (August 1991), 355-378.

     Catharine MacKinnon's arguments on law and sexual harassment are the basis of this article. Minson challenges MacKinnon's attempt to synthesize social theory and legal reform strategies related to SH. Specific areas addressed include the sociology of sex roles and tort law.

15. Minson, Jeffrey, ed. *Questions of Conduct: Sexual Harassment, Citizenship, Government.* New York: St. Martin's Press, 1993.

     Politics, social policy, government, and SH come together in this compilation of essays. Through these essays, the contributing authors explore the ethical and legal dimensions of SH, and how it relates to aspects of citizenship.

16. Norris, James M. "A comprehensive theory of sexual harassment in the organization." Dissertation, Michigan State University, 1985.

17. Paul, Ellen Frankel. "Bared buttocks and federal cases." *Society* 28:4 (May/June 1991), 4-7.

     Disagreeing with common assertions concerning SH, this author argues that the incidence of SH in the workplace has been greatly exaggerated and has turned into a highly charged ideological issue. A thick skin is necessary to survive in the workplace and women need to "lighten up" when it comes to trivial offenses. The author also argues that SH cases should not be handled under Title VII, but rather as torts. The kinds of undesired sexual behaviors women should be protected against by law are suggested.

18. Peirce, Michelle Ridgeway. "Sexual harassment and Title VII- A better solution." *Boston College Law Review* 30:4 (July 1989), 1071-1101.

The author asserts that there are serious analytical problems in treating SH as gender discrimination through the use of Title VII. Peirce maintains that forcing these cases into a framework of gender discrimination fails to address situations such as bisexual harassment or harassment in a single-sex environment.

19. Pollack, Wendy. "Sexual harassment: Women's experience vs. legal definitions." *Harvard Women's Law Journal* 13 (Spring 1990), 35-85.

The relationship between gender hierarchy and SH is the focus of this article. After reviewing several court cases, the author contends that SH policies and management training are not enough; recognition of and response to gender hierarchy is also necessary.

20. Pryor, John B., Christine M. LaVite, and Lynnette M. Stoller. "A social psychological analysis of sexual harassment: The person/situation interaction." *Journal of Vocational Behavior* 42:1 (February 1993), 68-83.

This paper introduces a social psychological framework for the scientific study of SH based on Pryor's Likelihood to Sexually Harass Scale (LSH) and Malamuth's self-report methodology for rape tendencies. Situational factors including local norms, and individual factors, including the linking of social dominance and sexuality by men, were found to contribute to SH in the workplace. The authors believe that SH behaviors can be studied under laboratory conditions so that situational and individual factors can be controlled. (47 refs).

21. Rhode, Deborah L. "Sexual harassment." *Southern California Law Review* 65:3 (March 1992), 1459-1466.

Rhode explores several forms of denial that are representative of popular responses to SH and other gender issues. These denial responses include: it didn't happen; if it happened then the woman is responsible; and it happened but it doesn't matter.

22. Rizzo, Ann-Marie, and Dolores Brosnan. "Critical theory and communication dysfunction: The case of sexually ambiguous behavior." *Administration & Society* 22:1 (May 1990), 66-85.

The authors explore several approaches which have been used to study SH, including feminist, legal, and organizational. These approaches act as a backdrop for comparing the structural-functional and critical theory perspectives of SH. Types of communication distortion are described in relationship to SH. (28 refs).

23.   Sepler, Fran. "Sexual harassment: From protective response to proactive prevention." *Hamline Journal of Public Law and Policy* 11:1 (Spring 1990), 61-78.

This article examines SH from sociological and legal perspectives. The author describes how differently SH is viewed across institutional and professional boundaries. The economic, physical, and psychological consequences of SH are presented as are a number of preventive strategies to promote eradication of SH in organizations.

24.   Stockdale, Margaret S. "The role of sexual misperceptions of women's friendliness in an emerging theory of sexual harassment." *Journal of Vocational Behavior* 42:1 (February 1993), 84-101.

The author discusses the tendency of some men to perceptually distort women's friendly behavior as sexual behavior and how this misperception relates to existing theories of SH. Attitude and belief-system variables affect the degree of distortion, as do situational factors. Influences for predicting certain forms of SH are provided. (60 refs).

25.   Superson, Anita M. "A feminist definition of sexual harassment." *Journal of Social Philosophy* 24:1 (Spring 1993), 46-64.

SH, the author points out, is about domination and, in particular, the domination of the group of men over the group of women. The objective definition of SH presented by Superson has as its primary benefit that it recognizes the harmful effects of SH on all women. Various feminist arguments regarding the sexual nature of SH are discussed.

26.   Terpstra, David E., and Douglas D. Baker. "A framework for the study of sexual harassment." *Basic and Applied Social Psychology* 7:1 (March 1986), 17-34.

Terpstra and Baker describe a theoretical framework for the study of SH based on causal factors, SH behaviors, individual responses, and organizational consequences. Existing research is examined to support their proposed framework. (83 refs).

27.   Thacker, Rebecca A., and Gerald R. Ferris. "Understanding sexual

harassment in the workplace: The influence of power and politics within the dyadic interaction of harasser and target." *Human Resource Management Review* 1:1 (Spring 1991), 23-37.

The authors introduce a framework that examines the behavior of harassers and their targets by focusing on the power and political relationships between the two parties. The model covers both the type of harassment perpetrators will exhibit as well as victim response. (39 refs).

28. Vaux, Alan. "Paradigmatic assumptions in sexual harassment research: Being guided without being misled." *Journal of Vocational Behavior* 42:1 (February 1993), 116-135.

Several assumptions regarding gender-related violence paradigms are explored. The author argues that these paradigms have both misled as well as guided SH research. Unresolved problems in SH research and an alternative view of SH are discussed. (66 refs).

29. Webb, Susan L. *Shockwaves: The Global Impact of Sexual Harassment.* New York: MasterMedia Limited, 1994.

The global pervasiveness of SH is explored by Webb in this publication. Webb uses "global" to refer to the pervasiveness of SH; it is everywhere and impacts all of humanity. Included are geographical sketches, a directory of service organizations, and a bibliography of print and nonprint resources.

30. Weeks, Elaine Lunsford, Jacqueline M. Boles, Albeno P. Garbin, and John Blount. "The transformation of sexual harassment from a private trouble into a public issue." *Sociological Inquiry* 56:4 (Fall 1986), 432-455.

The authors address the role of various social forces and groups whose interaction have brought SH to the forefront of the public agenda. Those examined include: the media, interest groups, and the courts. (68 refs).

31. Wekesser, Carol, Karin L. Swisher, and Christina Pierce, eds. *Sexual Harassment.* San Diego, CA: Greenhaven Press, 1992.

As part of the Current Controversies series, this book provides answers to four complex SH questions: 1) Is SH a serious problem? 2) What causes SH? 3) How can SH be reduced? 4) Can broad legal definitions of SH be effectively used in the courts? Contributing authors present a wide range of political and philosophical approaches for examining SH.

2

Perceptions of Males and Females Toward Sexual Harassment

32.   Baker, Douglas D., David E. Terpstra, and Kinley Larntz. "The influence of individual characteristics and severity of harassing behavior on reactions to sexual harassment." *Sex Roles* 22:5/6 (March 1990), 305-325.

   One hundred forty-three male and 100 female college students participated in this study of reactions to 18 scenarios which depicted a range of behaviors from innocuous to overt SH. Findings revealed that the perceived severity of the SH situations strongly influenced reactions. Individual factors such as gender, religiosity, and locus of control influenced reactions to a lesser degree, with gender having the strongest effect of these factors. (73 refs).

33.   Baker, Douglas D., David E. Terpstra, and Bob D. Cutler. "Perceptions of sexual harassment: A re-examination of gender differences." *Journal of Psychology* 124:4 (July 1990), 409-416.

   In a self-report survey of 409 state government employees, the existence of gender differences in the perception of SH was examined. These employee perceptions, when compared to those of a previous study of student perceptions, indicate fewer gender differences than organizational differences. Also, workers were more likely to perceive some incidents as more severe than students. (17 refs).

34.   Bartling, Carl A., and Russell Eisenman. "Sexual harassment proclivities in men and women." *Bulletin of the Psychonomic Society* 31:3 (May 1993), 189-192.

   In an effort to determine whether women as well as men have proclivities to sexually harass, the authors administered their newly

developed Sexual Harassment Proclivities Scale (SHPS) to 60 male
and 162 female college students. Correlations with related scales were
generally high, with the SHPS shown to be both reliable and valid.
Of the findings, the personality profiles for those likely to sexually
harass appeared to be similar for men and women. (14 refs).

35.   Bingham, Shereen G., and Brant R. Burleson. "Multiple effects of
       messages with multiple goals: Some perceived outcomes of responses
       to sexual harassment." *Human Communication Research* 16:2 (Winter
       1989), 184-216.

       The authors describe their study of 360 male and 217 female college
       students which explored the effectiveness of messages delivered in
       response to SH situations. The messages were examined according to
       O'Keefe's "design logic" and "goal structure". Respondents found none
       of the messages more effective than the others at stopping SH
       behavior. (43 refs).

36.   Booth-Butterfield, Melanie. "Perception of harassing communication as a
       function of locus of control, work force participation, and gender."
       Communication Quarterly 37:4 (Fall 1989), 262-275.

       The author describes the results of her study of college students and
       working adults which examined the influence of locus of control and
       gender on the perception of sexually harassing communication.
       Findings included, for example, that locus of control appeared to
       influence men more than women, that women labeled more behaviors
       SH than did men, and that workers perceived behaviors as sexually
       harassing more often than did students. (60 refs).

37.   Burian, Barbara Katrina. "Group composition and judgments of sexual
       harassment (gender composition)." Dissertation, Southern Illinois
       University, 1990.

38.   Campbell, Julie Lynne. "Male faculty attitudes toward and tolerance for
       sexual harassment (women)." Dissertation, Ohio University, 1990.

39.   Castellow, Wilbur A., Karl L. Wuensch, and Charles H. Moore. "Effects
       of physical attractiveness of the plaintiff and defendant in sexual
       harassment judgments." *Journal of Social Behavior and Personality* 5:5
       (November 1990), 547-562.

       Seventy-one male and 74 female students at East Carolina University
       participated in a study which examined how the physical attractiveness
       of the plaintiff can affect decision making in determining guilt and
       innocence in SH claims. The combination of attractive plaintiff and

unattractive defendant rendered more guilty judgments. Implications for jury trials are offered. (34 refs).

40.   Cleveland, Jeanette N., and Melinda E. Kerst. "Sexual harassment and perceptions of power: An under-articulated relationship." *Journal of Vocational Behavior* 42:1 (February 1993), 49-67.

The authors define power and explain how it comes into play in cases of SH. They argue that power plays a larger role in quid pro quo SH than in hostile environment SH, although it does not provide a full explanation for the occurrence of SH. Two areas of further research are suggested: the measurement of the specific aspects of power and SH, and a more systematic investigation between the individual differences among harassers and non-harassers. (77 refs).

41.   Cohen, Aaron Groff, and Barbara A. Gutek. "Dimensions of perceptions of social-sexual behavior in a work setting." *Sex Roles* 13:5/6 (September 1985), 317-327.

Two hundred three undergraduates read vignettes depicting a single social-sexual interaction between a man and a woman at work. Participants' answers to follow-up questions suggest that more weight is placed on the personal aspects of the incident rather than the possibility of SH. (20 refs).

42.   Fitzgerald, Louise F., and Matthew Hesson-McInnis. "The dimensions of sexual harassment: A structural analysis." *Journal of Vocational Behavior* 35:3 (December 1989), 309-326.

As a follow-up to Fitzgerald and Shulman, et al. (1988), an adaptation of the Sexual Experiences Questionnaire (SEQ) was utilized in this study of 28 college students. Factors that influence individuals' perceptions of SH were investigated and included: degree of severity of SH, the type of SH (quid pro quo vs. work conditions), and the form of coercion (physical vs. psychological). Results found that the structure of SH requires at least 2 dimensions (type and severity) to account for the data, and that the continuum of severity model is an oversimplification. Application of such a study in the workplace is also examined. (35 refs).

43.   Gehlauf, DeeAnn N., and Paula M. Popovich. "The effects of personal and situational factors on university administrators' responses to sexual harassment." *Research in Higher Education* 35:3 (June 1994), 373-386.

In a study of 195 university administrators' responses to SH scenarios, no sex differences in perceptions and definitions of SH were found although they were found in complaint handling and belief in SH myths. Suggestions for further research are offered. (19 refs).

44.   Gruenewald, Douglas Kent. "An analysis of student perceptions of sexual harassment by faculty at Iowa State University." Dissertation, Iowa State University, 1993.

45.   Harris, Jewell Bachtler. "Development of an operational definition of sexual harassment in higher education." Dissertation, University of Alabama, 1990.

46.   Hartnett, John J., David Robinson, and Betsy Singh. "Perceptions of males and females toward sexual harassment and acquiescence." *Journal of Social Behavior and Personality* 4:3 (1989), 291-298.

Two studies of college students were conducted to examine the perceptions of 60 male and 95 female subjects to hypothetical SH scenarios. In the first study, the subjects read a description of a SH incident without any indication of the outcome of the incident. In the second study, the victim gave in to the demands of the harasser. Subjects did not appear to make differential perceptions of the harasser or victim on the basis of gender, and generally agreed on their disciplinary recommendations regardless of the subject's gender. (15 refs).

47.   Horgan, Dianne D., and Glenn Reeder. "Sexual harassment." *American Association of Occupational Health Nurses Journal* 34:2 (February 1986), 83-86.

Undergraduates from psychology classes participated in this study which examined three aspects of hypothetical SH situations: the reward structure, the victims' behavior/decision-making, and the gender of the victim. Scenarios were presented in which subjects rated various details on an 11 point scale. The author uses attribution theory to show how the beliefs of the observer, the characteristics of the victim, and aspects of the situation can affect the viewer's perception of the victim. (8 refs).

48.   Jaschik, Mollie L., and Bruce R. Fretz. "Women's perceptions and labeling of sexual harassment." *Sex Roles* 25:1/2 (July 1991), 19-23.

This study of 90 female college students examined the hypothesis that women are not likely to label behaviors as SH without being cued to do so. After viewing video scenarios which contained either no, subtle, or explicit SH, subjects completed measures of perceptions.

While the subjects perceived SH in the appropriate videos, most did not initially label it as such. The authors contend these results indicate one reason why SH goes unreported. (12 refs).

49.　Johnson, Catherine B., Margaret S. Stockdale, and Frank E. Saal. "Persistence of men's misperceptions of friendly cues across a variety of interpersonal encounters." *Psychology of Women Quarterly* 15:3 (September 1991), 463-475.

This study examined the strength of gender differences in SH perception when male-female roles are reversed, when social interactions become sexually harassing, and when the response was either accepting or rejecting. One hundred eighty-seven female and 165 male undergraduates viewed a video which depicted 12 scenarios. Male subjects tended to view the female victim as behaving in a more sexual manner than female subjects, regardless of the victim's response. (28 refs).

50.　Johnson, Kim K. P., and Jane E. Workman. "Clothing and attributions concerning sexual harassment." *Home Economics Research Journal* 21:2 (December 1992), 160-172.

Johnson and Workman describe a survey of 200 college students which investigated the effects of provocative clothing on both provoking SH and of being sexually harassed. The clothing variable was controlled through the use of photographs. The Student-Newman-Keuls test was used to analyze the results. Participants rated the model in provocative clothing significantly higher on the likelihood of provoking SH. (21 refs).

51.　Jones, Gwendolyn. "Attitudes toward and perceptions of sexual harassment in the workplace." Dissertation, University of Washington, 1987.

52.　Jones, Tricia S., Martin S. Remland, and Claire C. Brunner. "Effects of employment relationship, response of recipient and sex of rater on perceptions of sexual harassment." *Perceptual and Motor Skills* 65:1 (August 1987), 55-63.

Seventy-six male and 82 female undergraduates were administered questionnaires which investigated three possible variables in the perception of SH: employment relationship, response to the recipient, and the sex of the rater. Results indicated that only the response of the recipient and the sex of the rater affected subjects' perceptions. (29 refs).

53.   Jones, Tricia S., and Martin S. Remland. "Sources of variability in perceptions of and responses to sexual harassment." *Sex Roles* 27:3/4 (August 1992), 121-142.

Using social exchange theory, the authors propose an explanation of the effects of gender, SH severity, and target responses to SH on perceptions of SH. In their study of undergraduates (94 male and 116 female), results indicated that all of these variables affected perceptions of SH situations. (31 refs).

54.   Konrad, Alison M., and Barbara A. Gutek. "Impact of work experiences on attitudes toward sexual harassment." *Administrative Science Quarterly* 31:3 (September 1986), 422-438.

Three theories are proposed by the authors to explain individual differences in perceptions and attitudes toward SH: men and women define SH differently, work experiences affect attitudes and perceptions of SH, and gender role "spillover" occurs in traditional male or female jobs. A telephone survey of 1,232 working men and women in Los Angeles County provided some support for each of the theories. (29 refs).

55.   Lancaster, Kelly O'Neal. "Conflict management in situations of sexual harassment: An exploratory study." Dissertation, University of Oklahoma, 1986.

56.   Liotta, Richard F. "The effects of perpetrator and victim physical attractiveness and history of incest on attribution of blame and responsibility in sexual harassment." Dissertation, Depaul University, 1988.

57.   Lloyd, Elizabeth Hagy. "An analysis of the relationship of men and women's educational attainment and gender to their perceptions of sexual harassment." Dissertation, University of Virginia, 1984.

58.   Luo, Tsun-Yin. "Sexual harassment and sexual assault: University students' attitudes towards sexual victimization of women." Dissertation, University of Hawaii, 1991.

59.   Maddox, Setma L. Reinhard. "Perceptions of sexual harassment." Dissertation, The University of Texas at Arlington, 1993.

60.   Milner, Laura M. "Factors influencing the perception of sexual harassment." Dissertation, Kansas State University, 1985.

61.   Neale, Norah Cathleen. "The role of culture and gender in perceptions of sexual harassment." Dissertation, University of Minnesota, 1992.

62.   Nocera, Romy. "The identification of factors leading to perceptions of sexual harassment in academia: A policy capturing approach." Dissertation, Bowling Green State University, 1992.

63.   Olsen, Eric R. "Sexual harassment proclivity of men: Relationship to values." Dissertation, Oregon State University, 1992.

64.   Pollack, David Michael. "Variables affecting perceptions of social-sexual situations as sexual harassment in the workplace." Dissertation, Bowling Green State University, 1988.

65.   Popovich, Paula M., DeeAnn N. Gehlauf, Jeffrey A. Jolton, Jill M. Somers, and Rhonda M. Godinho. "Perceptions of sexual harassment as a function of sex of rater and incident form and consequence." *Sex Roles* 27:11/12 (December 1992), 609-625.

The purpose of this study was to examine the perceptions of the severity dichotomies implicit in EEOC Guidelines by presenting 99 male and 99 female undergraduates with statements based on the guidelines. In the statements, the type of SH (physical vs. verbal) and the consequence of SH (economic vs. hostile environment) were varied. Both groups rated the "economic injury" statement as having a greater effect on the victim's job status than the hostile environment statement. Results also indicated that males viewed incidents less negatively than females and perceived incidents as more likely to be based on attraction than on power. (25 refs).

66.   Powell, Gary N. "Effects of sex role identity and sex on definitions of sexual harassment." *Sex Roles* 14:1/2 (January 1986), 9-19.

Powell explores the effects of sex, sex role identity, and the interaction between the two on definitions of SH. Two hundred forty-nine undergraduate students and 102 employed graduate students were administered the Bem Sex-Role Inventory and classified as high or low in masculinity or femininity. While gender of the rater was a strong factor in defining SH, sex-role identity had only a minor effect. The masculinity of both male and female subjects also affected definitions. (20 refs).

67.   Pryor, John B. "The lay person's understanding of sexual harassment." *Sex Roles* 13:5/6 (September 1985), 273-286.

In an attempt to examine how lay people interpret behavior as SH, 36 undergraduates completed a SH rating of 24 scenarios. An attributional theory model was used to analyze those factors that contributed to their defining certain behaviors as SH. Subjects acknowledged more influence from the social role variables than their perceptions of the target and perpetrator. Also, the perception of the behavior appeared to be influenced by the context in which the behavior occurred. (30 refs).

68.   Pryor, John B. "Sexual harassment proclivities in men." *Sex Roles* 17:5/6 (September 1987), 269-290.

This article describes the development and validation of the Likelihood to Sexually Harass (LSH) Scale, which uses 10 scenarios of male-female interactions with varying power discrepancies. Subjects indicated how they would respond to the situations if there would be no negative consequences. Three separate studies of male college students found that the likelihood of such behavior can be reliably measured by the LSH, and that the LSH can be used to provide a partial profile of men who are likely to harass. (47 refs).

69.   Pryor, John B., and Jeanne D. Day. "Interpretations of sexual harassment: An attributional analysis." *Sex Roles* 18:7/8 (April 1988), 405-417.

In an attempt to replicate and extend earlier research which used the attributional model of sexual harassment judgments, two studies were conducted to investigate: 1) how gender of the rater can affect perceptions of an event; and 2) how the physical characteristics of the female target can affect perceptions of an event. These studies indicate that SH judgments are strongly related to attributions of causality. (22 refs).

70.   Remland, Martin S., and Tricia S. Jones. "Sex differences, communication consistency, and judgments of sexual harassment in a performance appraisal interview." *Southern Speech Communication Journal* 50:2 (Winter 1985), 156-176.

The authors describe their study involving social exchange theory and the formation of judgments about sexual harassment in which speech communication students judged communication behavior between a superior and subordinate. Female judges were found to be more disapproving of the perpetrator than were male judges. (40 refs).

71.   Rubin, Linda Jo. "Sexual harassment: Individual differences in reporting behaviors." Dissertation, University of Kansas, 1992.

72.   Saal, Frank E., Catherine B. Johnson, and Nancy Weber. "Friendly or sexy? It may depend on whom you ask." *Psychology of Women Quarterly* 13:3 (September 1989), 263-276.

The authors describe the results of three studies which support Abbey's (1982) finding that men tend to perceive more sexual motives, such as flirting or seductiveness, in women's behavior than women perceive. The findings suggest that misperceptions should be considered in SH research models. (21 refs).

73. Sheffey, Susan, and R. Scott Tindale. "Perceptions of sexual harassment in the workplace." *Journal of Applied Social Psychology* 22:19 (October 1992), 1502-1520.

This article describes a study, based on the sex-role spillover model of SH, which was designed to assess the effects of the work setting on perceptions of SH. Two hundred thirty-four college students at Loyola University- Chicago read scenarios which took place in 3 different types of work settings: female-dominated, male-dominated, and mixed. Ambiguous behaviors were perceived as being more harassing in male-dominated or mixed settings than in female-dominated settings. (31 refs).

74. Shotland, R. Lance, and Jane M. Craig. "Can men and women differentiate between friendly and sexually interested behavior?" *Social Psychology Quarterly* 51:1 (1988), 66-73.

Following a review of the existing literature concerning gender differences in the differentiation between friendly and sexually interested behavior, the authors report the results of their related study of college students. Males in this study were more likely to perceive behaviors as sexually interested than females. (29 refs).

75. Sigler, Robert T., and Ida M. Johnson. "Public perceptions of the need for criminalization of sexual harassment." *Journal of Criminal Justice* 14:3 (1986), 229-237.

A survey of 144 residents of Tuscaloosa, Alabama investigated their perceptions of SH. Significant findings included reports of victimization at least as great on the streets and public places as in the workplace, and that blacks and women endorsed criminal legislation for SH at higher levels than did whites and men. The environment in which SH occurred also affected the endorsement for legislation.

76. Smith, Douglas Dale. "The efficacy of a selected training program on changing perceptions of sexual harassment." Dissertation, University of Northern Colorado, 1993.

77.   Tata, Jasmine. "The structure and phenomenon of sexual harassment: Impact of category of sexually harassing behavior, gender, and hierarchical level." *Journal of Applied Social Psychology* 23:3 (February 1993), 199-211.

The author reports results of a study which investigated the impact of three factors on an individual's perception of SH: the categories of SH behavior, the gender of subjects, and the hierarchical position of the initiator. Undergraduates (50 male and 70 female) were asked to assess 15 incidents dealing with social-sexual behaviors in an organizational setting. Respondent gender and initiator status influenced the perception of the less severe forms of SH, but not the more severe forms. (26 refs).

78.   Terpstra, David E., and Douglas D. Baker. "A hierarchy of sexual harassment." *Journal of Psychology* 121:6 (November 1987), 599-605.

A hierarchy of harassment was developed based on the responses of 48 working women and 243 students (143 males and 100 females) to 18 scenarios representing a wide range of SH behaviors. Results showed some differences between the perceptions of working women and female students, with a greater number of working women considering the behaviors to be SH. (11 refs).

79.   Terpstra, David E., and Douglas D. Baker. "Psychological and demographic correlates of perception of sexual harassment." *Genetic, Social, and General Psychology Monographs* 112:4 (November 1986), 461-478.

Terpstra and Baker describe the results of their survey of 243 students (143 males and 100 females) at Washington State University. The relationship between students' perceptions of SH and variables such as self-esteem, religion, and locus of control is explored. Results indicate that an individual's perception of SH is a function of his/her cognitive appraisal of social-sexual behaviors, but is also influenced by gender. (49 refs).

80.   Thacker, Rebecca A., and Stephen F. Gohmann. "Male/female differences in perceptions and effects of hostile environment sexual harassment: "Reasonable" assumptions?" *Public Personnel Management* 22:3 (Fall 1993), 461-472.

Data from the 1987 survey of federal employees conducted by the U.S. Merit Systems Protection Board was analyzed and used to explore gender differences in perceptions of reasonableness and psychological distress. Results of this study suggest that gender differences in these areas are significant. Not only are females more likely to define certain behaviors as sexually harassing, they are also more likely to need emotional or medical counseling as a result of experiencing such behaviors. (20 refs).

81.   Thomann, Daniel A., and Richard L. Wiener. "Physical and psychological causality as determinants of culpability in sexual harassment cases." *Sex Roles* 17:9/10 (November 1987), 573-591.

This article describes a study in which 196 college students were presented hypothetical scenarios detailing a harassment event in which three variables were manipulated: 1) flagrancy of request; 2) response of the victim; and 3) frequency of similar encounters. The students then completed questionnaires designed to determine how observers of behaviors decide culpability and disciplinary action in cases of alleged SH. Findings indicate that as the accused harasser's requests became more frequent, observers were more likely to perceive the incident as constituting SH. Results are examined from a hierarchical legal perspective. (43 refs).

82.   Williams, Karen B., and Ramona R. Cyr. "Escalating commitment to a relationship: The sexual harassment trap." *Sex Roles* 27:1/2 (July 1992), 47-72.

Sixty male and 60 female college students participated in this study which explored how SH perceptions are affected by a perpetrator's gradual sexual advancements and a target's escalating commitment to their relationship. Results supported the idea that males focus on the behavior of the target while females focus on the behavior of the perpetrator. (41 refs).

83.   Williams-Quinlan, Susan. "Intergenerational attitudes and beliefs about sexual assault and sexual harassment (rape myths)." Dissertation, University of Rhode Island, 1990.

84.   Workman, Jane E., and Kim K. P. Johnson. "The role of cosmetics in attributions about sexual harassment." *Sex Roles* 24:11/12 (June 1991), 759-769.

The study investigated perceptions concerning SH and the use of cosmetics. Seventy-six male and 85 female college students viewed photos of a model wearing either heavy, moderate, or no cosmetics. Subjects then indicated how likely the model was to provoke SH or to be harassed. Findings revealed that when the model wore heavy or moderate cosmetics, she was rated more likely to be harassed than when she wore no cosmetics. (28 refs).

85.   York, Kenneth M. "Defining sexual harassment in workplaces: A policy-capturing approach." *Academy of Management Journal* 32:4 (December 1989), 830-850.

The author asked 79 equal employment opportunity officers and 15 university students to judge 80 incidents of SH to determine if they were severe enough to file an EEOC complaint. Both groups relied on three aspects when making judgments: victim reaction, existence of coercion, and job consequences. (29 refs).

3

Physical, Psychological, and Economic Consequences of Sexual Harassment

86. Bingham, Shereen Gay. "Interpersonal responses to sexual harassment." Dissertation, Purdue University, 1988.

87. Bryan, Penelope E. "Holding women's psyches hostage: An interpretive analogy of the Thomas/Hill hearings." *Denver University Law Review* 69:2 (January 1992), 171-200.

    Bryan's essay presents an analogy between war prisoners' reactions to captivity and women's responses the Thomas-Hill hearings. The trauma experiences by POWs and the trauma inflicted on women by the Senate Judiciary Committee are discussed. A loss of important support and justice systems as well as the transformation of the status from person to object are cited as negative aspects of both experiences.

88. Bursten, Ben. "Psychiatric injury in women's workplaces." *Bulletin of the American Academy of Psychiatry and the Law* 14:3 (1986), 245-251.

    With the accelerating presence of women in the workplace has come increasing reports of problems they encounter because they are women. The author emphasizes that the psychiatric consequences of SH are sharper and more pronounced than the consequences of problems such as lower pay. The author uses 3 case studies of females who have claimed psychiatric injury as a result of sexually offensive behaviors in the workplace.

89. Correa, Maria Judith. "Blame and stigmatization of victims of sexual and nonsexual harassment as a function of severity of harassment, of filing a grievance, and of consequences to the perpetrator (sexual harassment)." Dissertation, Florida State University, 1994.

90.   Crull, Peggy, and Marilyn Cohen. "Expanding the definition of sexual harassment." *Occupational Health Nursing* 32:3 (March 1984), 141-145.

This report illustrates the more subtle manifestations of SH and points out how they, like the quid pro quo situation, infringe on the woman's economic security, productivity, and health. The kinds of SH incidents reported to the Working Women's Institute are defined and categorized. How this information can be useful to those working in health-related fields is also included. (10 refs).

91.   Dandekar, Natalie. "Contrasting consequences: Bringing charges of sexual harassment compared with other cases of whistleblowing." *Journal of Business Ethics* 9:2 (February 1990), 151-158.

This article discusses the differences between SH charges and other more general whistleblowing charges against wrongful corporate practice. An examination of the underlying causes of these differences can provide insight into the practice of whistleblowing in a democratic society. (13 refs).

92.   Fitzgerald, Louise F. "Sexual harassment: Violence against women in the workplace." *American Psychologist* 48:10 (October 1993), 1070-1076.

Even though no true epidemiological studies have been done, large-scale surveys of working women indicate that nearly 1 out of every 2 women will be harassed while in school or at the workplace. Legislative proposals are presented, as well as primary prevention initiatives for psychologists working in the area of SH. (88 refs).

93.   Goldfarb, Rosalind G. "Effects of a workshop designed to promote effective coping with sexual harassment and its associated effects: A single case design ("N of one" study)." Dissertation, University of Maryland, 1985.

94.   Gruber, James E., and Lars Bjorn. "Women's responses to sexual harassment: An analysis of sociocultural, organizational, and personal resource models." *Social Science Quarterly* 67:4 (December 1986), 814-826.

Using a survey of female blue-collar workers, the authors tested three models- sociocultural, organizational, and personal resource models- for predicting response differences to SH. The organizational model provided two important factors for predicting response to SH (work area sex composition and job skills) as did the personal resource model (self-esteem and life satisfaction). (42 refs).

95.   Gutek, Barbara A., and Mary P. Koss. "Changed women and changed organizations: Consequences of and coping with sexual harassment." *Journal of Vocational Behavior* 42:1 (February 1993), 28-48.

The consequences of SH on women and organizations are examined, as are victim responses to SH. These responses include: individual responses, coping by the victim and others, and contingencies in response to SH. Due to lack of research literature on the topic of consequences of SH, the authors suggest areas of future research, including studies of the variables that determine the impact of SH and investigations into the true costs of SH lawsuits. (67 refs).

96.   Hamilton, Jean A., Sheryle W. Alagna, Linda S. King, and Camille Lloyd. "The emotional consequences of gender-based abuse in the workplace: New counseling programs for sex discrimination." *Women and Therapy* 6:1/2 (Spring/Summer 1987), 155-182.

The consequences of gender-based discrimination in the workplace, particularly SH, are the focus of this article. The authors refer to their review of legal, sociological, and psychological literature as well as to their clinical experience with victims of such discrimination. Symptomology related to DSM III ratings, effects on the family, the emotional consequences of the reporting process, and treatment guidelines are discussed. (59 refs).

97.   Harder, Vicki Jean. "Sexual harassment: Employee reactions and organizational consequences." Dissertation, Marquette University, 1994.

98.   Honstead, Mary Lou. "Correlates of coping methods of sexually harassed college students." Dissertation, University of Minnesota, 1987.

99.   Ito, Randy. "Beyond hostility." *Employee Assistance: Solutions to the Problems* 5:5 (1992), 13-16.

Ito advocates the use of employee assistance providers in dealing with workplace SH. Their active role and responsibilities are outlined.

100.   Kaplan, Sally J. "Consequences of sexual harassment in the workplace." *Affilia* 6:3 (Fall 1991), 50-65.

Previous research is used to examine the costs of SH to individuals, organizations, and society. Weaknesses of current social policy and recommendations for alleviating the economic consequences of SH are discussed. (26 refs).

101.   Kramer, Kevin Thomas. "Relief for health-related injury in sexual harassment cases." *Journal of Contemporary Health Law and Policy* 6 (Spring 1990), 171-191.

Remedies for health-related SH claims available under Title VII and alternative methods to obtain monetary awards are discussed in this article. Suggestions for needed changes in SH laws which will allow plaintiffs to recover damages for their health-related injuries are provided.

102.   Kulak, Marcia Sweeney. "Sexual harassment in the workplace: A claim perspective and interpretation." *CPCU Journal* 45:4 (December 1992), 227-233.

Kulak traces the development of SH law and assesses the impact of SH litigation on company and personal insurance policies. As the Civil Rights Act of 1991 allows victims more avenues for recourse, the author speculates that employers and accused individuals will increasingly turn to their insurance companies for protection. (5 refs).

103.   Loy, Pamela Hewitt, and Lea P. Stewart. "The extent and effects of the sexual harassment of working women." *Sociological Focus* 17:1 (January 1984), 31-43.

Five hundred and nine male and female residents of Connecticut participated in a telephone survey which investigated the frequency and types of SH, and their responses to SH. Findings included: 1) women were more likely than men to believe that harassment was a problem; 2) women tended to experience more undesirable personal outcomes rather than organizational outcomes; 3) women tended to deal with the harassment informally; and 4) supervisors and peers were most frequently cited as harassers. (16 refs).

104.   McDonald, James J., Jr., and Sara P. Feldman-Schorrig. "The relevance of childhood sexual abuse in sexual harassment." *Employee Relations Law Journal* 20:2 (Autumn 1994), 221-236.

Attorney McDonald and psychiatrist Feldman-Schorrig demonstrate that childhood sexual abuse can have a significant impact upon the victim's psychological profile and the manner in which she receives sexual cues later in life. Because of this possible impact, the authors argue that discovery into a history of childhood sexual abuse on the part of a plaintiff in a SH case should not be limited.

105. Nicks, Sandra Diana. "Responses to pervasive sexual harassment as a function of organizational grievance procedures, type of harassment, and status of harasser (grievances)." Dissertation, Saint Louis University, 1993.

106. Salisbury, Jan, Angela B. Ginorio, Helen Remick, and Donna M. Stringer. "Counseling victims of sexual harassment." *Psychotherapy* 23:2 (Summer 1986), 316-324.

   Actual clinical experiences with SH victims in individual (n=10) and group psychotherapy (n=7) settings were compared with data derived from both SH surveys and crime victim population data. The comparison found that many of the same symptoms, attitudes, and behaviors were exhibited by all groups. SH tends to affect economic and career well-being primarily, and private relationships and physical well-being secondarily; the reverse is true for victims of crime. When comparing treatments, groups psychotherapy was shown to be more effective than individual therapy, especially during initial stages of the SH experience. (42 refs).

107. Shrier, Diane K. "Sexual harassment and discrimination. Impact on physical and mental health." *New Jersey Medicine* 87:2 (February 1990), 105-107.

   The author discusses the widespread prevalence and serious economic, psychiatric, and stress-related health consequences of SH. She recommends referral of victims to mental health professionals with SH expertise and provides a list of women's resources concerning SH. (13 refs).

108. Spratlen, Lois Price. "Sexual harassment counseling." *Journal of Psychosocial Nursing and Mental Health Services* 26:2 (February 1988), 28-33.

   Investigative psychotherapy, used by the author as an approach to counseling SH victims, is defined and discussed. This approach as part of an informal grievance procedure at a major university. The therapist leads the client through a 3-step process to assess the client's needs, strengths, and problems. An extensive verbal exchange takes place between client and therapist, the client provides a written description of the SH incident, and a conciliation conference occurs with the alleged harasser. This process of problem solving leads to competency building and leads away from self-blame and loss of self-esteem. (17 refs).

109. Star, Kelly Gillmore. "The effects of sexual harassment on performance." Dissertation, California School of Professional Psychology, 1984.

110.   Terpstra, David E. "Organizational costs of sexual harassment." *Journal of Employment Counseling* 23:3 (September 1986), 112-119.

As a means of examining the potential organizational costs of SH, Terpstra surveyed 71 working women from two universities regarding their likely reactions to various forms of SH. Many reported they would quit their jobs or turn to external authorities to report the SH. The costs involved in both reactions are discussed. (15 refs).

111.   Terpstra, David E., and Douglas D. Baker. "The identification and classification of reactions to sexual harassment." *Journal of Organizational Behavior* 10:1 (January 1989), 1-14.

In an effort to identify and classify potential reactions to SH, 142 male and 100 female undergraduates and 44 working women were read 18 scenarios depicting some form of SH of a woman by a man. The subjects then wrote down what their response would be if they were in the woman's place. Sixty percent of the reactions fell into three categories: ignore it/do nothing, report the incident internally, or confront the harasser verbally. Comparisons of the reactions between men and women students, and between working women and women students, revealed few significant differences. (27 refs).

112.   Thacker, Rebecca A. "A descriptive study of behavioral responses of sexual harassment targets: Implications for control theory." *Employee Responsibilities and Rights Journal* 5:2 (1992), 155-171.

This article reports on an investigation of the efficacy of two personal control theories, reactance theory and learned helplessness theory, as a means of explaining victim response to SH. In a review of 59 SH cases, victim response typically followed one of three patterns: reactance only, reactance followed by learned helplessness, or learned helplessness. Findings are examined as are implications for organizations and future research directions. (51 refs).

113.   Whitfield, Charles L. "Denial of the truth: Individuals and political dysfunction in the Thomas-Hill hearings." *Journal of Psychohistory* 19:3 (Winter 1992), 269-279.

Psychotherapist Whitfield suggests that the Thomas-Hill hearings showed us that U.S. politicians are dysfunctional and in denial about the nature of sexual trauma and abuse. Reasons for the denial and misunderstandings surrounding this SH claim are presented. Reasons why Whitfield and his colleagues believed Anita Hill are also included.

114. Woody, Robert Henley, and Nancy Walker Perry. "Sexual harassment victims: Psycholegal and family therapy considerations." *American Journal of Family Therapy* 21:2 (Summer 1993), 136-144.

The author describes the psychological effects of SH (the sexual harassment trauma syndrome) on both the victim and the victim's family, and offers guidance for effective family therapy. Family therapy is considered the treatment of choice by this author for rebuilding the systemic strengths that are needed to promote the psychological health of the SH victim. (25 refs).

4

Organizational Culture and the Pervasiveness of Sexual Harassment

115. Bails, Constance Thomasina. "Females reaction to sexual harassment in the workplace and the impact of rape." Dissertation, Temple University, 1994.

116. Baridon, Andrea P., and David R. Eyler. *Working Together: The New Rules and Realities for Managing Men and Women at Work.* New York: McGraw-Hill, 1994.

    Although Baridon and Eyler explore a broad range of social-sexual interactions between men and women in the workplace, one issue discussed throughout the book is SH. From SH guidelines and policies to on-the-job etiquette, the authors provide approaches to solving the problems faced by men and women working together.

117. Cates, Jo. "Sexual harassment: What every woman and man should know." *Library Journal* 110:12 (July 1985), 23-29.

    Cates provides a snapshot of SH- the definitions, the laws, the harassers, the victims, and the courts. She provides information for harassed males and includes a list of support agencies available to all victims of SH. (51 refs).

118. Cooper, Kenneth C. "The six levels of sexual harassment." *Management Review* 74 (August 1985), 54-55.

    Cooper outlines six levels of SH based on the remarks of hundreds of SH victims discussing harassing situations. The levels are: aesthetic appreciation, active groping, social touching, foreplay harassment, sexual abuse, and ultimate threat.

119. Dhooper, Surjit Singh, Marlene B. Huff, and Carrie M. Schultz. "Social
      work and sexual harassment." *Journal of Sociology and Social Welfare*
      16:3 (September 1989), 125-138.

      Using a questionnaire developed by Maypole, the authors surveyed 97
      members of the Kentucky Chapter of the National Association of
      Social Workers concerning the incidence, type, and nature of SH in
      their places of employment. Results found that 26% of the
      respondents had been victims of SH; 51% knew of incidents of SH of
      other social workers. Young employees from small agencies and with
      few years of employment considered SH a serious problem. (5 refs).

120. Dolcheck, Maynard M. "Sexual harassment of Southern women in the
      workplace-- A problem that must be faced." *Mississippi Business
      Review* 46 (August 1984), 3-7.

      The author reviews his two previous studies of men and women with
      business degrees. These studies indicated that SH is a serious problem
      for organizations in the South. Organizational policies and complaint
      procedures are discussed. (12 refs).

121. Estrich, Susan. "Sex at work." *Stanford Law Review* 43 (April 1991),
      813-861.

      After a review of the rules and prejudices of traditional rape law
      currently used in SH cases, the author suggests several changes that
      the courts and Congress should adopt to make the laws work for
      women, not against them. Recommendations include: elimination of
      the welcomeness inquiry, burden of proof shifted to the harasser, and
      an encouragement of class actions.

122. Fain, Terri C., and Douglas L. Anderton. "Sexual harassment:
      Organizational context and diffuse status." *Sex Roles* 17:5/6
      (September 1987), 291-311.

      Using data from the 1981 U.S. Merit Systems Protection Board SH
      study, the authors investigated the effects of three factors on the
      general occurrence of SH in the workplace: power differentials, sex
      ratios within work groups, and diffuse master status or stereotypical
      responses from the community. Results indicated that diffuse status is
      a substantial determinant of SH and must be considered with power and
      sex ratios. (40 refs).

123. Feary, Vaughana Macy. "Sexual harassment: Why the corporate world
      still doesn't "get it"." *Journal of Business Ethics* 13:8 (August 1994),
      649-662.

Feary believes that SH in the workplace is not simply a
communication, gender, or cultural problem, but rather a moral
problem for everyone in the corporate world. A historical overview of
workplace SH is presented, followed by an outline of reasons for the
legal prohibition of SH and moral education of employees.

124. Filipczak, Bob. "Is it getting chilly in here? Men and women at work."
      Training 31:2 (February 1994), 25-30.

      Filipczak discusses what he believes to be icy relationships between
      the sexes in the workplace as a result of recent SH litigation. Several
      authors in the field of gender differences present their theories regarding
      SH, SH policy development, corporate power struggles, and
      communication techniques.

125. Foegen, J. H. "The double jeopardy of sexual harassment." *Business and
      Society Review* :82 (Summer 1992), 31-35.

      This article addresses the question, "Will men ignore their women
      coworkers?". The author asserts that the new awareness of SH risks
      the development of a chilled workplace atmosphere. Differences in
      gender perception are discussed.

126. Ford, Robert C., and Frank McLaughlin. "Sexual harassment at work:
      What is the problem?" *Akron Business and Economic Review* 20:4
      (Winter 1989), 79-92.

      An analysis of several empirical studies of SH was performed to
      examine the pervasiveness and types of harassing behaviors that are
      present in the workplace. Comments, innuendo, and sexual remarks
      are the types of SH which occurred most frequently. (37 refs).

127. Glass, Becky L. "Workplace harassment and the victimization of women."
      Women's Studies International Forum 11:1 (1988), 55-67.

      A survey of 607 women aged 18 to 65 in Forsyth County, North
      Carolina, compared their experiences with unwanted sexual advances
      in various settings such as on the job, in school, and in public places.
      While SH was more frequent in the workplace, it did occur in all
      settings. The authors assert that the similarities across settings
      indicate that SH results from overall male dominance in society rather
      than specific workplace characteristics. (34 refs).

128. Gutek, Barbara A. *Sex and the Workplace: The Impact of Sexual Behavior
      and Harassment on Women, Men, and Organizations.* San Francisco:

Jossey-Bass, 1985.

Gutek, an acknowledged scholar in the area of sexual behavior and the workplace, presents the findings of several studies regarding the characteristics of both victims and harassers, the sex-role spillover perspective, and the subtle effects of sex at work. Written for organizational consultants, human resources personnel, and managers, this book offers suggestions for managing and eliminating the problem of SH at work.

129. Gutek, Barbara A., Aaron Groff Cohen, and Alison M. Konrad. "Predicting social-sexual behavior at work: A contact hypothesis." *Academy of Management Journal* 33:3 (September 1990), 560-577.

A survey of 1,232 working men and women examined the effects of opposite gender contact in the work environment, and how it affects social-sexual behaviors. Specifically, the authors looked at sexual harassment, nonharassing behaviors, and sexualization of the work environment. Among other findings, the authors report that the perception by women of sexual harassment was directly correlated with contact with the opposite gender. The authors suggest that organizations could begin to desexualize the work environment by establishing standards of dress, conduct, or language. (62 refs).

130. Judd, Peter, Stephen R. Block, and Constance L. Calkin. "Sexual harassment among social workers in human service agencies." *Arete* 10:1 (Spring 1985), 12-21.

A study of 112 social workers employed in human service agencies throughout Colorado examined the pervasiveness and effects of SH in their agencies. Findings indicated that 49% of females and 17% of males reported having been victims of SH, with a significant number reporting negative emotional effects.

131. Klein, Freada Ruth. "Sexual harassment in federal employment: Factors affecting its incidence, severity, duration and relationship to productivity (sex discrimination)." Dissertation, Brandeis University, F. Heller Graduate School for Advanced Studies in Social Welfare, 1984.

132. Lee, Lucienne A., and P. Paul Heppner. "The development and evaluation of a sexual harassment inventory." *Journal of Counseling and Development* 69:6 (July/August 1991), 512-517.

The Harassment Sensitivity Inventory (HSI), an 18-item instrument designed to measure sensitivity to the negative effects of male-to-female SH behaviors in the workplace, is described. Psychometric data was gathered from 133 males and females. Implications of this questionnaire for exploring individual attitudes toward SH are presented. (21 refs).

133. Levinson, Daniel R., and Maria L. Johnson. *Sexual Harassment in the Federal Government: An Update*. Washington, D.C.: U.S. Merit Systems Protection Board, 1988.

This report, an update to the Merit Systems Protection Board's 1980 landmark study, details the findings of a 1987 follow up survey. The nature and the extent of SH, employer response, and the financial impact of SH on the federal government are all discussed. Data from the current study mirrors in many ways data from the earlier study even though several positive changes have taken place. The report concludes with recommendations for reducing SH within the government and the 1987 survey questionnaire is appended.

134. Lipschultz, Jeremy Harris, and Michael L. Hilt. "Broadcast managers and the Tolerance for Sexual Harassment Inventory." *Journal of Social Behavior and Personality* 9:1 (March 1994), 141-152.

A questionnaire which included the Tolerance for Sexual Harassment Inventory was completed by 151 broadcast general managers and news directors to determine their attitudes toward SH. There were no statistically significant differences between broadcast managers and news directors. The overall score was clearly in the direction of intolerance for SH. (16 refs).

135. Maypole, Donald E. "Sexual harassment of social workers at work: Injustice within?" *Social Work* 31:1 (January/February 1986), 29-34.

A survey of 188 male and 131 female members of the Iowa Chapter of the National Association of Social Workers investigated the scope of SH in their agencies. The combined victimization rate for the men and women surveyed was 27%. Victim response was generally dependent on the status of the perpetrator: avoidance was commonly used when the perpetrator was a supervisor or administrator, defusion through joking or some other means when the perpetrator was a co-worker, and reason when the perpetrator was a client. Implications of these findings for organizations are offered. (19 refs).

136. McIntyre, Douglas I., and James C. Renick. "Developing public policy on sexual harassment." *San Jose Studies* 12:2 (September 1986), 32-45.

Data from two surveys of female employees of the state governments of Florida and Illinois are used to illustrate the significance of SH problems at state levels of government. Recommendations for public policy are presented.

137. Meadows, Kay Earlene. "A study of sexual harassment in the work place." Dissertation, Kansas State University, 1989.

138. Popovich, Paula M. "Sexual harassment in organizations." *Employee Responsibilities and Rights Journal* 1:4 (January 1988), 273-282.

Popovich reviews the definitions and typical situational characteristics of SH. She urges organizations and employers to take a proactive role in combating this problem. The provision of counseling and support to victims is encouraged, as are the establishment of policies prohibiting SH and the education of employees. (20 refs).

139. Puckett, Darlene Loretta. "Reactions to workplace sexual harassment as a function of gender, supervisory responsibilities, sex-role orientation, and just world beliefs (androgyny)." Dissertation, University of Florida, 1984.

140. Quinn, Robert E., and Patricia L. Lees. "Attraction and harassment: Dynamics of sexual politics in the workplace." *Organizational Dynamics* 13:2 (Fall 1984), 35-46.

The authors examine two issues of interest which emerged from their research concerning intimacy at work- sexual attraction and SH. While behavior changes can take place when an intimate relationship develops at work, problems occur when power and rewards become distorted. The areas of co-worker harassment, SH of males by females, and false accusations are discussed. (7 refs).

141. Robinson, Robert K., Delaney J. Kirk, and James D. Powell. "Sexual harassment: New approaches for changed environment." *Advanced Management Journal* 52 (Autumn 1987), 15-18, 47.

Following a review of the *Meritor v. Vinson* case, the authors report results of their survey of business and professional women in which 71% of the respondents indicated they had been sexually harassed at work. Suggestions for reducing employer liability are offered.

142. Robinson, W. LaVome, and Pamela Trotman Reid. "Sexual intimacies in psychology revisited." *Professional Psychology Research and Practice* 16:4 (August 1985), 512-520.

The authors discuss the results of their SH study involving 287 female psychologists. In this study, they asked the subjects about SH experiences both as college students and as professional psychologists. Subjects reported more experiences of the lesser forms of SH than actual sexual contact, with both types of SH occurring more often during their schooling than during employment. Most respondents indicated that the experiences had a negative impact on one or both persons involved. (10 refs).

143. Savitzky, Lynn R. "A structural analysis of sexual harassment at work (sex-roles)." Dissertation, Claremont Graduate School, 1986.

144. Segrave, Kerry. *The Sexual Harassment of Women in the Workplace, 1600 to 1993.* Jefferson, NC: McFarland & Co., Inc., 1994.

From the indentured servant to the professional woman, Segrave chronicles the history of workplace SH. There are chapters covering trades and blue-collar workers, clerical workers, professionals, domestic workers, and litigation. The author provides information from global sources, although the emphasis of this publication is on SH in the United States.

145. Watstein, Sarah Barbara. "Disturbances in the field: Sexual harassment and libraries." *Wilson Library Bulletin* 67:9 (May 1993), 31-34.

Watstein explores SH in library literature and provides an overview of American Library Association initiatives in this area. A basic review of SH definitions, types of harassment typically seen in libraries, and employer liability issues are also included.

146. Weeks, Elaine Lunsford. "Sexual harassment as a workplace contingency." Dissertation, University of Georgia, 1988.

147. "What you told the world." *Executive Female* 15 (January/February 1992), 51, 53.

This brief article reports results of a telephone survey of 1,300 National Association of Female Executives. One of the findings was that 53% of respondents reported they or someone they knew had been sexually harassed.

148. Woods, Robert H. "Gender discrimination and sexual harassment as experienced by hospitality-industry managers." *Cornell Hotel and Restaurant Administration Quarterly* 35:1 (February 1994), 16-21.

The authors, faculty members at two schools of hotel and restaurant management, report results of their survey of 613 hospitality managers regarding SH and sexual discrimination. Findings indicated that 80% of male respondents and 90% of female respondents believe that sexual discrimination occurs frequently. Recommendations for educators are provided.

149. York, Kenneth M. "Sexual harassment in the workplace: A policy capturing approach." Dissertation, Bowling Green State University, 1986.

5

Sexual Harassment in Historically Traditional Male Occupations

150. Angel, Marina. "Sexual harassment by judges." *University of Miami Law Review* 45:4 (March 1991), 817-841.

      The author examines the SH of lawyers, law students, defendants, and court personnel by judges. She reports that sanctions against judges have been disproportionately low compared to the magnitude of the problem. The Model Code of Judicial Conduct, adopted by the American Bar Association in an effort to eliminate this type of behavior, is also discussed.

151. Arriola, Elvia R. ""What's the big deal?" Women in the New York City construction industry and sexual harassment law, 1970-1985." *Columbia Human Rights Law Review* 22:1 (July 1990), 21-71.

      The author asserts that the social and legal concept of SH grew out of, and reflects, the politics of gender that surfaced with the "women's liberation movement" of the 1970's. Events such as the opening of the Working Women's Institute, the *Redbook* survey, early SH court cases, and the increased national coverage of these cases are discussed.

152. Baker, Nancy Lynn. "Sexual harassment and job satisfaction in traditional and nontraditional industrial occupations." Dissertation, California School of Professional Psychology, 1989.

153. Brown, Robert, Jr., and Marjorie Van Ochten. "Sexual harassment: A vulnerable area for corrections." *Corrections Today* 52:5 (August 1990), 62, 64, 66, 68, 70.

      Brown, director of the Michigan Department of corrections, and Van

Ochten, an attorney, push for SH to be on the legal agenda for correction agencies. Women employed in this traditionally male field may experience SH from inmates or co-workers. Clear SH policies and training are suggested.

154. Burleigh, Nina, and Stephanie B. Goldberg. "Breaking the silence; sexual harassment in law firms." *ABA Journal* 75 (August 1989), 46-51.

This article examines the irony that most law firms fail to take their own advice concerning personnel training and written procedures to prevent SH complaints. Presents arguments for and against women lawyers reporting SH.

155. Committee on Women in the Profession. "Sexual harassment in the lawyers' workplace." *The Record of the Association of the Bar of the City of New York* 46:7 (1991), 728-754.

This article is based on a 1990 SH panel discussion sponsored by the American Bar Association's Special Committee on Women in the Profession. Committee members explored issues related to the SH of female lawyers. Recommendations for preventing SH, reporting and investigating complaints, and taking appropriate actions are provided.

156. Gilberd, Kathleen. "Sexual harassment in the military." *National Lawyers Guild Practitioner* 49:2 (Spring 1992), 38-54.

The author suggests that because the American military has always been perceived as a male environment, several factors unique to the military make SH particularly difficult to eradicate. The author offers a few avenues of redress available to servicewomen subjected to SH. (62 refs).

157. Gurney, Joan Neff. "Not one of the guys: The female researcher in a male-dominated setting." *Qualitative Sociology* 8:1 (Spring 1985), 42-62.

The author describes the variety of obstacles faced by female researchers in male-dominated settings. She believes that literature providing advice for the novice researcher in a field setting may be appropriate for males, but inappropriate for females due to sex-role expectations of others. SH, sexist jokes, and other sexist treatments are common dilemmas in these settings. Suggestions for managing and overcoming such problems are offered. (33 refs).

158. Honigsberg, Peter Jan, Marilynn Tham, and Gary Alexander. "When the client harasses the attorney- Recognizing third-party sexual harassment

in the legal profession." *University of San Francisco Law Review* 28:3 (Spring 1994), 715-737.

The authors examine issues related to the SH of women attorneys by clients. Legal protections for third party SH, power dynamics involved in such circumstances, and the importance of well-articulated law firm policies against SH are discussed.

159.   Kesselman, Amy V. "Women shipyard workers in Portland and Vancouver during World War II and reconversion (Washington, OR)." Dissertation, Cornell University, 1985.

160.   Krohne, Kathleen Ann Quinn. "The effect of sexual harassment on female naval officers: A phenomenological study." Dissertation, University of San Diego, 1991.

161.   Lafontaine, Edward, and Leslie Tredeau. "The frequency, sources, and correlates of sexual harassment among women in traditional male occupations." *Sex Roles* 15:7/8 (October 1986), 433-442.

The authors examine results of a survey of 160 women in non-traditional occupations. This survey revealed that 75% of respondents had experienced at least one form of SH, vs. 50% of women cited for the general population. Peers were the most frequently cited sources of harassment. The findings are also discussed within the framework of patriarchy. (16 refs).

162.   Lindquist, Jeffery C. "Sexual harassment in the military: Can Article 93, UCMJ, meet the challenge?" *Journal of Legal Studies (USAFA)* 4 (1993), 59-73.

Given the increasing number of women in the military, it is logical to assume that reports of SH may also increase. One means of dealing with SH in the military is Article 93, Uniform Code of Military Justice. Lindquist offers an historical examination of Article 93, discusses its use by military courts, and argues that it can be used to effectively fight SH in the armed forces.

163.   Majka, Linda C. "Sexual harassment in the Church." *Society* 28:4 (May/June 1991), 14-21.

The responses of clergy and students concerning SH attitudes and experiences are reported on in this article, part of a national survey conducted by the United Methodist Church. The findings indicated that both groups often experienced unwanted sexual attention and that they view SH as part of a larger realm of social problems.

164. Mangione-Lambie, Mary Giselle. "Sexual harassment: The effects of
      perceiver, gender, race, and rank on attitudes and action." Dissertation,
      The California School of Professional Psychology- San Diego, 1994.

165. Mansfield, Phyllis Kernoff, Patricia Barthalow Koch, Julie Henderson,
      Judith R. Vicary, Margaret Cohn, and Elaine W. Young. "The job
      climate for women in traditionally male blue-collar occupations." *Sex
      Roles* 25:1/2 (July 1991), 63-79.

      The work environments of two groups of women workers in
      traditionally male blue-collar occupations were studied: tradeswomen
      (n=71) and transit workers (n=151). School secretaries (n=389) were
      studied to provide a comparison group of women in a traditionally
      female occupation. Results indicated that high levels of SH were
      directed at women in traditionally male occupations, and that they
      experienced more stressful work conditions and were significantly less
      satisfied than those in the comparison group. (32 refs).

166. Martindale, Melanie. "Sexual harassment in the military: 1988."
      Sociological Practice Review 2:3 (July 1991), 200-216.

      A 1988 survey of 20,400 active military personnel investigated their
      perceptions of SH as well as their experiences. Sixty-four percent of
      the female respondents and 17% of the male respondents had
      experienced some form of SH at least once in the year prior to the
      survey. Victims tended to be younger and did not report the incidents.
      Even though they felt their leaders to be aware of SH policies and had
      made attempts to curtail SH, most of the respondents were unaware of
      remedies for victims or penalties against perpetrators.

167. McEnery, Jean. "Sexual harassment in blue-collar jobs- A problem
      unresolved." *Employment Relations Today* 11:2 (Summer 1984), 205-
      215.

      The study described in this article utilized two focus groups and a
      questionnaire to identify the incidence and types of SH experienced by
      women in blue collar jobs out in the field. One finding indicated that
      both on-the-job training and the work environment posed a great
      number of problems for these women. (10 refs).

168. Meier, Jody. "Sexual harassment in law firms: Should attorneys be
      disciplined under the lawyer codes?" *Georgetown Journal of Legal
      Ethics* 4:1 (Summer 1990), 169-188.

      This five-part article illustrates the problems associated with SH in
      law firms. Part one defines SH, part two describes SH in the law firm

environment, and parts three and four discuss liability issues. In part five, the author argues that state bar disciplinary boards should use already existing professional rules of behavior to discipline partners who sexually harass associates.

169. Niebuhr, Robert E., and Wiley R. Boyles. "Sexual harassment of military personnel: An examination of power differentials." *International Journal of Intercultural Relations* 15:4 (1991), 445-457.

Data from previous studies were analyzed to determine if patterns of SH differed among racial or ethnic groups in the military. The independent variables included were: victim's office or enlisted classification, gender, marital status, and harasser's race. Findings concluded, for example, that nonwhite female officers reported less SH than white female officers. (20 refs).

170. Rasnic, Carol. "Illegal use of hands in the locker room: Charges of sexual harassment and inequality from females in the sports media." *Entertainment and Sports Lawyer* 8:4 (Winter 1991), 3-8.

The presence of female reporters in the locker room of male athletes is the focus of this article. The author contends that compromises such as a deferral of all interviews until players have dressed would prevent the SH of female reporters and protect the privacy of athletes. (41 refs).

171. Timmins, William M., and Brad E. Hainsworth. "Attracting and retaining females in law enforcement: Sex-based problems of women cops in 1988." *International Journal of Offender Therapy and Comparative Criminology* 33:3 (December 1989), 197-205.

This article describes a survey of 541 female police officers concerning the reasons why they began and have remained in police work, and which sex-based problems they have experienced at work. Findings indicate that significant numbers of these women have encountered SH. (8 refs).

172. White, Pamela J. "Model policies condemn sexual harassment by legal employers." *The Maryland Bar Journal* 26:2 (March/April 1993), 40-43.

The author provides a review of startling survey results and court cases which indicated that SH is indeed a problem in the legal workplace. The American Bar Association drafted a sample SH policy and guidelines to serve as a starting point for lawyers. Excerpts from these guidelines are included.

173. Wong, Molly Mo-Lan. "Sexual harassment at work: Female police officers." Dissertation, University of Pittsburgh, 1984.

174. Yount, Kristen R. "Ladies, flirts, and tomboys: Strategies for managing sexual harassment in an underground coal mine." *Journal of Contemporary Ethnography* 19:4 (January 1991), 396-422.

Following a 5-month field experiment, three distinctive gender role adaptations were found to be used by women to manage SH in coal mines. Female coal miners chose a role adoption as either a lady in which men were viewed as gentlemen, as a flirt in which they interacted with men in a manner viewed as seductive, or as a tomboy in which they identified heavily with the work role as coal miner. The negative impact of each role is discussed and implications for educational programs are provided. (27 refs).

6

Sexual Harassment of Medical Professionals and Trainees

175. Arbeiter, Jean S. "Sexual harassment: You *can* do something about it." *RN* 49:10 (October 1986), 46-51.

 Due to the hierarchical nature of hospitals, the author asserts that they are natural breeding grounds for SH. In an informal survey about SH by doctors, co-workers, and patients, nearly one RN in five reported having been harassed.

176. Arbeiter, Jean S. "Stopping sexual harassment: The experts tell you how." *RN* 49:10 (October 1986), 51-55.

 Three experts on SH provide advice to victims on how to stop SH in health care settings. They suggest a variety of approaches for dealing with this issue and, if none of these suggestions work, advise the victim to contact the local civil rights agency, the EEOC, or the courts. A list of organizations that fight SH is also provided.

177. Baldwin, DeWitt C., Jr., Steven R. Daugherty, and Edward J. Eckenfels. "Student perceptions of mistreatment and harassment during medical school. A survey of ten United States schools." *Western Journal of Medicine* 155:2 (August 1991), 140-145.

 Senior students at 10 medical schools were surveyed regarding the frequency with which they had experienced different types of perceived mistreatment or harassment over the course of medical school, as well as the source of that perceived mistreatment. A response rate of 59% yielded more than half of the students reporting some form of SH.

The biggest SH complaints were sexist slurs and favoritism in terms of grades or attention. (25 refs).

178.   Brushwood, David B. "Hospital and pharmacist liability for sexual harassment of a pharmacy technician." *American Journal of Hospital Pharmacy* 51:3 (February 1, 1994), 397-399.

The author, an attorney and professor of pharmacy health care administration, presents the 1992 case of *Ridge v. HCA Services of Kansas, Inc.*, as the backdrop for his primer on SH law. Brushwood is quick to point out that firm action by hospital pharmacy management is vital, with supervising pharmacists at risk for increased liability if their conducts leads to hospital liability.

179.   Bullough, Vern L. "Nightingale, nursing and harassment." *Image: Journal of Nursing Scholarship* 22:1 (Spring 1990), 4-7.

Explores the physical, emotional, and mental challenges nursing students dealt with in the nineteenth century, one of the most common of which was SH. Illustrates Florence Nightingale's concern for these nursing students and their steps taken to avoid the problems of SH. (19 refs).

180.   Cardinale, Val. "Sexual harassment on the job." *Drug Topics* 136 (March 9, 1992), 39.

Cardinale reports the results from a survey of 1,036 community and hospital pharmacists investigating the prevalence of SH in the pharmaceutical workplace. Results indicated that 26% of respondents have either experienced SH or know someone who has. Also, more chain pharmacists than independent or hospital pharmacists reported personal SH experiences.

181.   Chiodo, Gary T., Susan W. Tolle, and Daniel Labby. "Sexual advances by patients in dental practice: Implications for the dental and dental hygiene curricula." *Journal of Dental Education* 56:9 (September 1992), 617-624.

The authors, after a review of related research, describe a survey of dentists and dental hygienists investigating the frequency and type of patient-initiated sexual advances they had experienced in a five year period. Of the 483 respondents, up to 44% of them had experienced one or more verbal advances and up to 23% reported one or more physical advances. Implications for dental education are included. (37 refs).

182. Cholewinski, Jane T., and Janet M. Burge. "Sexual harassment of nursing students." *Image: Journal of Nursing Scholarship* 22:2 (Spring 1990), 106-110.

   The purpose of this study was to investigate the frequency and type of SH experienced by nursing students, their perceptions of the effects of these experiences on academic performance, and the resources used by students to assist in coping with the experience. The sample consisted of 277 subjects but discussion of results is confined to a subset of 21 students. Verbal abuse and sexist remarks were the most common types of SH. Although most students reported no initial effect on their academic performance, some students reported an increased inability to concentrate on their academic work. More than half of the subjects discussed their SH experiences with friends of the same sex. The authors offer several suggestions for further research regarding SH of nursing students. (10 refs).

183. Colantonio, Connie. "Brandon didn't know his limits." *NursingLife* 4:2 (March/April 1984), 34-35.

   The author describes Brandon, a head nurse who sexually harassed other nurses on his medical/surgical unit. No action was taken against him until a serious patient injury occurred. The nurses finally supported each other to take action against Brandon. Methods of discouraging potential harassers are also included.

184. Cotton, Paul. "Harassment hinders women's care and careers." *JAMA* 267:6 (February 12 1992), 778-779, 783.

   The author explores recent SH cases in various university, governmental, and medical facilities in which female medical professionals have experienced SH. He quotes healthcare and legal experts who stress the importance of SH prevention, sensitivity, and increased awareness of the problems facing women in medical facilities.

185. Creighton, Helen. "Sexual harassment: Legal implications- Part II, Nursing." *Nursing Management* 18:7 (July 1987), 16,18.

   The author focuses on the SH problem in nursing and explores legal cases illustrating the financial impact on the productivity of nurses and their hospitals as a result of SH. (13 refs).

186. Dernocoeur, Kate, and James N. Eastman, Jr. "Have we really come a long way? Women in EMS survey results." *Journal of Emergency Medical Services* 17:2 (February 1992), 18-19.

A 1991 survey of women in emergency medical services (EMS) showed SH in the workplace to be a pressing issue. Of the 199 respondents, 44% reported SH experiences. When asked to describe the harassment, 18% cited inappropriate comments, 7% cited sexist attitudes, 7% said they had been touched inappropriately, and 4% said they been the target of sexual advances. Respondents agreed that management should be trained in discrimination and harassment issues.

187.   Diaz, Anne L., and J. Daniel McMillin. "A definition and description of nurse abuse." *Western Journal of Nursing Research* 13:1 (February 1991), 97-109.

Abusive behavior is defined here as the behavior of one person which, through words, tone, manner, or other nonverbal cues, uses the power of a dominant position inappropriately toward a subordinate. A random sample of 164 female RNs were surveyed as to any unfavorable interactions with physicians. The types and frequencies of abuse are reported, including 30% of respondents indicating they had experienced some form of sexual abuse at least once every 2-3 months and 64% reporting that they had been verbally abused by a physician at least once every 2-3 months. Consequences of these abusive interactions are explored. (17 refs).

188.   Dowell, Marsha. "Sexual harassment in academia: Legal and administrative challenges." *Journal of Nursing Education* 31:1 (January 1992), 5-9.

The impact of SH on nursing students is addressed, as is the need for nurse administrators to be knowledgeable about university SH policies and procedures. (42 refs).

189.   Garvin, Cynthia, and Salli Harris Sledge. "Sexual harassment within dental offices in Washington State." *Journal of Dental Hygiene* 66:4 (May 1992), 178-184.

This study examined the extent of SH problems in dental offices in the state of Washington. A random sample of registered dental hygienists yielded a return rate of 72.6%. Results indicated that 26.3% of respondents had personally experienced one or more forms of SH in their work settings. Over half of those respondents indicated they had been harassed by dentists/employers, and 37.1% reported harassment by patients; 8% reported harassment by coworkers and others. (17 refs).

190.   Genovich-Richards, Joann. "A poignant absence: Sexual harassment in the health care literature." *Medical Care Review* 49:2 (Summer 1992),

133-159.

Focusing on the nursing literature, the author examined nine medical
journals from 1980 to 1990 for articles on SH. Of the 94 articles, the
author suggests that few articles were actually substantive and of value
to American health care professionals. (97 refs).

191.   Gervasi, Rosetta. "Sexual harassment in the dental office: Results of
ADAA's nationwide survey." *Dental Assistant* 53:3 (May/June 1984),
25-29.

This article examines results of a nationwide survey of dental
assistants which indicated that SH is a serious problem in dentistry.
Included are methods used to deal with the SH, the demographic profile
of survey respondents, and excerpts from several personal anecdotes
received from respondents. (3 refs).

192.   Goldberg, Gayle L., and Janet Thompson Reagan. "Sexual harassment: A
problem for the health care supervisor." *Health Care Supervisor* 3:3
(April 1985), 55-65.

In the health care industry, where top level management and physicians
are usually male and the support staff in administration and patient care
are usually female, the likelihood of perceived and actual SH is
increased. A 1982 survey of RNs attending a program at Memphis
State University is described in detail. This survey revealed that 60%
of respondents had been subjected to SH within the past year and that a
serious consequence of SH was distraction of nurses from performing
their patient care duties. (43 refs).

193.   Gordon, Geoffrey H., Daniel Labby, and Wendy Levinson. "Sex and the
teacher-learner relationship in medicine." *Journal of General Internal
Medicine* 7:4 (July/August 1992), 443-447.

Women make up 40% of the first-year medical student population and
28% of the residency positions in the U.S. Consequently, female
students and residents work with a predominately male senior faculty.
In an attempt to enhance open discussion of teacher-learner sexual
behavior in medical training, the author discusses the major emotional
and lifestyle changes medical students and residents undergo.
Consensual sexual contact is explored as are the consequences for
learners involved in teacher-learner relationships. (17 refs).

194.   Grieco, Alan. "Scope and nature of sexual harassment in nursing." *Journal
of Sex Research* 23:2 (May 1987), 261-266.

Four hundred and sixty-two licensed nurses in Missouri completed a
questionnaire which investigated the prevalence of SH in nursing. The
author found that, overall, 76% of respondents had experienced some
form of SH, with 82% of the female respondents and 67% of the male
respondents reporting SH. Patients were cited most often as the
perpetrators (87%), followed by physicians (67%), and coworkers
(59%). (6 refs).

195.   Grieco, Alan. "Suggestions for management of sexual harassment of
       nurses." *Hospital and Community Psychiatry* 35:2 (February 1984),
       171-172.

       Several practical suggestions for the management of SH which evolved
       from a series of multidisciplinary ward meetings are reported on in this
       article. The author, asserting that prevention is the first line of
       defense, recommends: prompt charting of incidents involving patients
       and open discussion in ward rounds; identification of high-risk places
       such as private rooms or storerooms; the use of a buddy system when
       feasible; and role-playing. (7 refs).

196.   Griffin-Shelley, Eric. "Sexual harassment: One organization's response."
       Journal of Counseling and Development 64:1 (September 1985), 72-
       73.

       Eighteen male and 58 female employees of a psychiatric hospital
       responded to a survey which examined the prevalence of SH in their
       institution. Results indicated that 47% of female respondents had
       experienced some form of SH, with physicians and department heads
       the primary perpetrators. None of the males reported SH. (8 refs).

197.   Haim, Patricia. "Sexual harassment. Looking at the law." *Journal of the
       Oregon Dental Association* 61:3 (Spring 1992), 40-42.

       The author offers dentists practical advice concerning SH, which is
       considered unprofessional conduct and can lead to the suspension or
       revocation of a dentist's license . The definition of SH, liability, and
       policy development are covered, and a sample policy is included. (1
       ref).

198.   Heinrich, Kathleen T. "Effective responses to sexual harassment."
       Nursing Outlook 35:2 (March/April 1987), 70-72.

       The author discusses the SH Intervention Model, originally designed to
       help visiting nurses and other community health personnel assess and
       deal with SH in their practices. This approach addresses the nurse, the
       harasser, and the environmental setting in which the harassment takes

place. It provides for the formulation of intervention strategies which are: avoidance, exploration of motives, confrontation, and withdrawal of services. (5 refs).

199. Horsley, Jack E. "Don't tolerate sexual harassment at work." *RN* 53:1 (January 1990), 69, 72, 75.

This author is a strong proponent of speaking out against SH. Confronting the harasser in person and in writing, filing a written complaint with supervisors, administrators, and the EEOC are specific measures offered as a means of stopping SH.

200. Jordheim, Anne E. "What's the best way to handle a sexually aggressive patient?" *Journal of Practical Nursing* 36:4 (December 1986), 30-33.

Fifty female nurses enrolled in a human sexuality course were surveyed to determine how they handled male patients' sexual advances. Their overriding response was that a nurse's actions determined whether a patient would make a sexual advance. The nurses noted that religious men, drug addicts, and alcoholics were common sources of sexual advances. Strategies used to fend off sexual advances by patients are presented.

201. Julius, Daniel J., and Nicholas DiGiovanni, Jr. "Sexual harassment: Legal issues, implications for nurses." *AORN Journal* 52:1 (July 1990), 95-99, 101-104.

The author asserts that trends in SH cases point toward health care administrators being held liable for implementing internal grievance procedures and training programs. Administrative mechanisms to address SH and steps in the education of hospital personnel are given. (33 refs).

202. Kettl, Paul, James Siberski, Christine Hischmann, and Beverly Wood. "Sexual harassment of health care students by patients." *Journal of Psychosocial Nursing and Mental Health Services* 31:7 (July 1993), 11-13.

The purpose of the study described in this article was to determine the frequency and type of SH of health care students by patients in a psychiatric hospital. With 40% of respondents indicating they had been SH victims, the authors developed a training program on handling SH by patients. An outline of their SH program is included. (6 refs).

203. Komaromy, Miriam, Andrew B. Bindman, Richard J. Haber, and Merle A. Sande. "Sexual harassment in medical training." *New England Journal of Medicine* 328:5 (February 1993), 322-326.

This article describes a survey of 82 internal medicine residents (33 female and 49 male) which investigated whether they had encountered SH during medical school or residency, the frequency and type of SH, its effect on them, and whether they chose to report it. The authors found that 24 of the female and 11 of the males respondents reported experiencing at least one SH situation during their training. Only 2 women reported the SH even though 19 women and 5 men felt it created a hostile environment or had a negative impact on their work. Methods for addressing this problem are explored. (32 refs).

204. Lenhart, Sharyn A., Freada Klein, Patricia Falcao, Elizabeth Phelan, and Kevin Smith. "Gender bias and sexual harassment of AMWA members in Massachusetts." *Journal of the American Medical Women's Association* 46:4 (July 1991), 121-125.

A survey of the Massachusetts members of the American Medical Women's Association, assessed the extent to which they had experienced various forms of discrimination and unwanted sexual attention. Findings revealed that 54% of respondents had encountered some form of sex discrimination, with 27% reporting SH experiences over a one-year period. (5 refs).

205. Libbus, M. Kay, and Katherine G. Bowman. "Sexual harassment of female registered nurses in hospitals." *Journal of Nursing Administration* 24:6 (June 1994), 26-31.

A random sample of registered nurses licensed to practice in Missouri replied to a questionnaire about the frequency of SH in a hospital setting. A greater number of respondents reported experiencing SH from male patients than from male co-workers. Implications for nurse administrators are included. (18 refs).

206. Maurizio, Sandra J., and Janet L. Rogers. "Sexual harassment and attitudes in rural community care workers." *Health Values: The Journal of Health Behavior, Education and Promotion* 16:4 (July/August 1992), 40-45.

This study addressed training effectiveness on the attitudes toward and knowledge of SH of 735 community care workers in southern Illinois. An analysis of pretest and posttest data indicated that the training program was effective, with the largest change in attitude in the area of professional appearance. (13 refs).

207. Nora, Lois Margaret, Steven R. Daugherty, Keith Hersh, Jan Schmidt, and Larry J. Goodman. "What do medical students mean when they say "sexual harassment"?" *Academic Medicine* 68:10 Suppl. (October 1993), S49-S51.

The authors report results of a survey of 146 male and 160 female medical students in which their reactions to a set of 14 scenarios depicting possible medical school situations were analyzed. The students were asked to: rate the level of SH present in each scenario, assign each party a level of responsibility, and comment on each scenario. Results indicated that the students showed a high degree of consensus as to the rank order of behaviors that do or do not constitute SH. As with other similar surveys, the women tended to perceive a greater degree of SH in most scenarios than did the men. (6 refs).

208. Outwater, Lynn C. "Sexual harassment issues in home care: What employers should do about it." *Caring* 13:5 (May 1994), 54-56.

This article serves as a SH primer aimed specifically at the home health care employer. Because a home care employer can be liable for the conduct of its supervisors and employees, as well as its clients, their family members, or other third parties, the likelihood of SH charges in the home care business is very high. The prevention of SH, costs of SH, and victim profiles are discussed. (10 refs).

209. Pokalo, Cheryl L. "Verbal abuse and sexual harassment in the OR." *Today's OR Nurse* 13:9 (September 1991), 4-7.

The health care industry, in which 97% of the nurses are women and 83.6% of the doctors are men, has a history of harassment activity, the most common types being verbal abuse and SH. Common sense precautions for avoiding SH are provided. Documented SH by physicians should be reported by the hospital to the state board of medicine as such reports may ultimately be grounds for termination. (9 refs).

210. Ratliff, Marion S. "Sexual harassment: Your staff won't tell you but their attorney might." *Journal of the Oregon Dental Association* 61:3 (Spring 1992), 32-38.

Federal and state agencies concerned with SH violations are presented. One agency, the Oregon Board of Dentistry has received, on average, one SH complaint every two years from patients. In 1989 the Board added rules prohibiting SH of dental staff members. It receives an average of one complaint from staff per year. Differing frames of reference between men and women are discussed as are ways of resolving SH complaints.

211. Reiter, Colleen. "Sexual harassment in the dental practice." *Dental Assistant* 59:1 (January/February 1990), 16-19.

As the person who initiates SH is usually in a position superior to that of the victim, the harasser in the dental setting could be a dentist, a salesperson, or a patient. The dental assistant should be aware of potential SH situations and behaviors, and may want to consider one of the following responses to SH: document any inappropriate incidents and conversations, discuss the incidents with the harasser, file a formal complaint with a federal agency, or pursue the matter in court. A list of resource groups available to SH victims is offered. (5 refs).

212. Rogers, Janet L., and Sandra J. Maurizio. "Prevalence of sexual harassment among rural community care workers." *Home Healthcare Nurse* 11:4 (July/August 1993), 37-40.

This article discusses results of a survey of rural community care workers (CCWs) identifying the prevalence of SH at their various work sites. The authors found that over 27% of the CCWs were harassed on the job. Several recommendations are provided for educators dealing with these work settings. (11 refs).

213. Schunk, Carol, and Corrine Propas Parver. "Avoiding allegations of sexual misconduct." *Clinical Management in Physical Therapy* 9:5 (September/October 1989), 19-22.

Physical therapy treatment is often based on a hands-on approach to healing, more so than almost any other health care profession. Techniques such as massage, myofascial release, and sacroiliac joint mobilization may foster a patient's misrepresentation of the therapist's intent. These authors assert that by adopting a preventative posture, therapists will minimize the chance of a negative situation occurring.

214. Telles-Irvin, Patricia, and Ivy S. Schwartz. "Sexual harassment among female dentists and dental students in Texas." *Journal of Dental Education* 56:9 (September 1992), 612-616.

The authors were prompted to conduct a survey of SH among female dentists and dental students as a result of several incidents of SH that were reported by dental students at the authors' dental school. The 226 subjects reported a greater frequency of harassment by patients than by colleagues. Implications for dental educators and practitioners are presented. (25 refs).

215. Waring, Margaret B., and Marie Larmer Horn. "Sexual harassment:
      Prevention and legal aspects." *Dental Hygiene* 61:5 (May 1987), 206-
      211.

      Because most dental hygienists are female, the issue of SH is a very
      relevant in the dental environment. This article outlines the
      professional responsibilities of the dental employer, clarifies the
      victim's rights and avenues for recourse, and reviews the implications
      for dentistry in light of the EEOC Guidelines. The authors focus both
      on the need to train supervisors and managers as well as the inclusion
      of this topic in dental education curriculae. (21 refs).

216. Wizer, David R. "Sexual harassment in podiatric medical education. The
      residency interview process." *Journal of the American Podiatric
      Medical Association* 82:11 (November 1992), 590-593.

      The survey described in this article serves as a follow-up to an
      American Podiatric Medical Students' Association pilot study
      conducted in 1988 investigating SH during residency interviews. One
      hundred eighty residents participated in this study, of which 28
      reported experiencing some type of SH during the residency interview
      process. Recommendations based on these results are included. (4
      refs).

217. Wolf, T. M., H. M. Randall, K. Von Almen, and L. L. Tynes. "Perceived
      mistreatment and attitude change by graduating medical students: A
      retrospective study." *Medical Education* 25:5 (May 1991), 182-190.

      A class of graduating medical students were surveyed concerning the
      types and sources of perceived mistreatment during four years of
      medical education. Perceived mistreatment is discussed as it relates to
      attitude change and academic performance. Of the 61% of the students
      who responded, 98.9% reported mistreatment, with psychological
      mistreatment by residents/interns being most frequent. Over half of
      the students perceived some form of SH, with 80% of the harassment
      reported by residents/interns. The adverse effects of mistreatment are
      discussed with recommendations for improving medical education. (18
      refs).

218. Wolf, Thomas M., Philip L. Scurria, Angela B. Bruno, and John A.
      Butler. "Perceived mistreatment of graduating dental students: A
      retrospective study." *Journal of Dental Education* 56:5 (May 1992),
      312-316.

      This study assesses the frequency, types, and sources of perceived
      mistreatment during four years of dental education among a class of

graduating seniors. Of the 30 male and 8 female students who anonymously completed a mistreatment questionnaire, SH was perceived by about one-third of the students; 25% of the female students reported sexual advances, sexist teaching materials, and favoritism. (24 refs).

7

Employer Responsibility: Preventive and Corrective Actions

219. Aalberts, Robert J., and Lorne H. Seidman. "Sexual harassment by clients, customers, and suppliers: How employers should handle an emerging legal problem." *Employee Relations Law Journal* 20:1 (Summer 1994), 85-100.

    The authors offer a model policy for dealing with the SH of employees by non-employees such as customers and suppliers. Although few courts have addressed this issue, the authors base their model on the landmark case of *Robinson v. Jacksonville*.

220. Aaron, Titus, and Judith A. Isaksen. *Sexual Harassment in the Workplace: A Guide to the Law and a Research Overview for Employers and Employees*. Jefferson, NC: McFarland & Co., Inc., 1993.

    This book is an overview of SH in the workplace. Items of particular emphasis include: federal and state regulations, conduct which constitutes SH, and employer responsibilities and liabilities. A glossary and bibliography are included.

221. Acken, Brenda T., Kent St. Pierre, and Peter Veglahn. "Limiting sexual harassment liability. The best defense is an effective policy against harassment." *Journal of Accountancy* 171:6 (June 1991), 42-47.

    The authors contend that CPA firms are at risk even though males and females are employed at various management levels. Their argument is that the upper management positions are dominated by men, with very few women holding any of those positions. Appended is a sample policy against SH from any source, including clients.

222. Anderson, Katherine S. "Employer liability under Title VII for sexual harassment after *Meritor Savings Bank v. Vinson.*" *Columbia Law Review* 87:6 (October 1987), 1258-1279.

The author reviews various legal approaches to employer liability for SH and compares them to cases of non-sexual harassment. The author asserts that once SH is proven to be as unambiguously offensive and illegal as non-sexual discrimination, there is no reason to establish a different standard for the determination of employer liability.

223. Barker, Sally E., and Loretta K. Haggard. "A labor union's duties and potential liabilities arising out of coworker complaints of sexual harassment." *Saint Louis University Public Law Review* 11:1 (Spring 1992), 135-156.

Co-worker complaints of SH can be problematic for a union because it owes a duty of fair representation to all employees in the bargaining unit. The authors address this issue and recommend several steps unions can take to provide fair investigations and avoid liability.

224. Baxter, Ralph H. , Jr., and Lynne C. Hermle. *Sexual Harassment in the Workplace: A Guide to the Law.* New York: Executive Enterprises, 1994.

Now in its fourth edition, this guide to the law explores the current legal principles which govern SH cases. Baxter and Hermle, both legal specialists in employment counseling and litigation, provide detailed advice to managers and others who may face issues related to SH in their organization. Suggestions for limiting employer liability are offered. The work concludes with case and policy examples and selected readings.

225. Behrens, Curtiss K. "Co-worker sexual harassment: The employer's liability." *Personnel Journal* 63:5 (May 1984), 12, 14.

Discusses "just cause" disciplinary actions in both the union and non-union setting by briefly describing representative cases. (15 refs).

226. Bryson, Cheryl Blackwell. "The internal sexual harassment investigation: Self-evaluation without self-incrimination." *Employee Relations Law Journal* 15:4 (Spring 1990), 551-559.

Although it is of vital importance that SH claims be investigated and resolved quickly, the investigation should be carefully executed. The author takes the reader through each step to be considered when planning an investigation.

227. Burge, David J. "Employment discrimination-- Defining an employer's liability under Title VII for on-the-job sexual harassment: Adoption of a bifurcated standard." *North Carolina Law Review* 62 (April 1984), 795-811.

Burge analyzed three standards of employer liability adopted by the courts: 1) strict employer liability for supervisors' acts of SH; 2) employer liability when knowledge existed of SH but no action was taken; and 3) a bifurcated standard which treats supervisory actions different depending upon the conditions. In cases of hostile environment, SH by a supervisor is treated as SH by a peer. In cases of quid pro quo, the supervisor becomes an official agent of the employer, and those actions are thus treated as if with full knowledge of the employer.

228. Cohen, Cynthia Fryer, and Joyce P. Vincelette. "Notice, remedy, and employer liability for sexual harassment." *Labor Law Journal* 35:5 (May 1984), 301-307.

The authors contend that there are inconsistancies between the EEOC Guidelines and judicial decisions concerning employer liability. Implications of these inconsistancies are provided for both employees and employers.

229. Committee on Labor and Employment Law. "Law firm policies on workplace sexual harassment." *The Record of the Association of the Bar of the City of New York* 48:2 (March 1993), 179-193.

This report by the Committee on Labor and Employment Law focuses on the need for law firms to vigorously implement and enforce a SH policy. Practical reasons for and key elements of a SH policy are outlined. A model policy aimed specifically at law firms is included.

230. Connell, Dana S. "Effective sexual harassment policies: Unexpected lessons from Jacksonville Shipyards." *Employee Relations Law Journal* 17:2 (Autumn 1991), 191-206.

Although the EEOC and courts have offered very little guidance to employers regarding the elements of a comprehensive SH policy, the 1991 *Robinson v. Jacksonville Shipyards* decision does provide specific policy guidance. This article offers suggestions on how employers may adopt portions of the actual Jacksonville Shipyards policy, which appears as an appendix.

231. Corum, Michael. *Combating Sexual Harassment: Disciplining the Sexual Harasser.* Arlington, VA: Dewey Publications, Inc., 1993.

This book was written for those in management who are responsible for handling allegations or situations of SH and taking corrective action when warranted. The author presents detailed recommendations regarding investigating allegations, assessing credibility, choosing appropriate corrective actions, and applying disciplinary procedures.

232. DuRose, Richard A. "Sexual harassment turned on its head: Dealing with claims by the accused aggressor." *For the Defense* 32:1 (January 1990), 2-7.

This article explores several cases filed by employees who have been disciplined as a result of a SH accusation. These cases illustrate the value of a thorough investigation of the SH claim and the importance of considering a number of disciplinary actions.

233. Eubanks, Paula. "Preventive measures key to sexual harassment policies." *Hospitals* 65:22 (November 20 1991), 35-36.

Labor attorneys and hospital human resources experts provide insight into the prevention of SH in the hospital setting. Potential sources of legitimate SH claims in hospitals include: medical staff that harbor disrespect for nurses, operating rooms in which sexually abusive remarks are exchanged in tense moments, and workplace romances gone sour. Experts agree that a ban on SH must be supported by the medical staff, top management, and the board of directors. Information on crafting an effective SH policy for hospitals is also included.

234. Falkner, Robert F., and Mariann T. Spencer. "Practical guidelines to follow when confronted with an allegation of sexual harassment." *Corporate Counsel's Quarterly* 8:4 (October 1992), 142-145.

The authors present simple, step-by-step guidelines for employers to follow when confronted with a SH allegation. The suggestions range from assuring the complainant that there will be no retaliation to making an effort to curb any gossip related to the incident.

235. Frierson, James G. "Sexual harassment in the workplace costly in production, absenteeism, turnover." *Preventive Law Reporter* 8:2 (June 1989), 3-9.

After a brief overview of SH law, Frierson provides examples of SH policies as well as complaint forms to be used by employers when handling SH complaints.

236. Garvey, Margaret S. "The high cost of sexual harassment suits." *Personnel Journal* 65:1 (January 1986), 75-78,80.

In an effort to explain why employers should avoid liability in SH cases, the financial outcome of SH cases which went against the employer are discussed. Garvey stresses the need for educational programs, and presents employers a sample SH policy and checklist to avoid liability.

237.   Gilsdorf, Jeanette W. "Sexual harassment as a liability issue in communication." *Bulletin of the Association for Business Communication* 53:3 (September 1990), 68-77.

The author focuses on the causes of misunderstandings surrounding SH including mixed social and workplace roles, and nonmutual attraction. Methods of reducing the economic and emotional costs of SH are discussed, as are means to help ensure that employers will be free of liability. (49 refs).

238.   Goodyear, Mary Lou, and William K. Black. "Combating sexual harassment: A public service perspective." *American Libraries* 22:2 (February 1991), 134-136.

Co-authors of the Iowa State University Library's Policy on Harassment, Goodyear and Black provide examples of common SH scenarios in libraries, and describe the development and implementation of their anti-harassment policy and corresponding support system.

239.   Greenlaw, Paul S., and William H. Port. "Military versus civilian judicial handling of SH cases." *Labor Law Journal* 44:6 (June 1993), 368-374.

The differences and similarities between military and civilian judicial systems' treatment of SH cases are explored in this article. One difference discussed in detail is that military law is based on individual responsibility rather than employer responsibility as is the case with civilian law.

240.   Haggard, Thomas R. /Alexander, Mason G., Jr. "Tips on drafting and enforcing a policy against sexual harassment." *Industrial Management* 36:1 (January/February 1994), 2-5.

Haggard and Alexander offer suggestions for presenting a comprehensive, clearly written SH policy. Methods of providing interim relief for both the complainant and the accused are presented as well as recommendations for the final written report.

241.   Hallinan, Kathleen M. "Invasion of privacy or protection against sexual harassment: Co-employee dating and employer liability." *Columbia*

Journal of Law and Social Problems 26:3 (Spring 1993), 435-464.

At the same time employers are dealing with problems associated with SH in the workplace, they have been reluctant to confront the issue of co-worker dating. However, Hallinan contends that it is in the employer's best interest to develop a policy addressing this issue since behaviors can be become harassing once a relationship has ended. Dating restrictions in the public and private sectors are explored and a policy restricting dating between supervisors and their direct subordinates is proposed.

242.   Hames, David S. "An actionable condition of work-related sexual harassment." *Labor Law Journal* 43:7 (July 1992), 430-439.

Recent court decisions are used to illustrate what constitutes unlawful conduct and employer liability in the workplace. Discussed are issues related to gender, pervasiveness, discriminatory intent, and the nature of harassment. The author urges employers to increase their efforts to prevent the incidence of SH in the workplace.

243.   Jacoby, M. Elaine. "A guide to handling sexual harassment claims in the workplace." *Corporate Counsel's Quarterly* 8:2 (April 1992), 128-141.

Following a review of Title VII, employer liability, and recent court cases, this article turns to preventive and investigatory procedures involving both inside and outside counsel to handle SH complaints.

244.   Jensvold, Margaret F. "Workplace sexual harassment: The use, misuse, and abuse of psychiatry." *Psychiatric Annals* 23:8 (August 1993), 438-445.

Because incidents of SH and related grievance procedures sometimes cause emotional symptoms, psychiatrists and other mental health professionals often become involved. Both appropriate and inappropriate roles mental health professionals can play are discussed. Appropriate roles include: as therapists, as expert witnesses in courts, and as psychological evaluators of plaintiffs. Unethical behaviors include: breaches of confidentiality to third-parties and the threat of forced psychiatric evaluations to intimidate plaintiffs. Guidelines for mental health practitioners are presented. (26 refs).

245.   Johnson, Margaret E. "A unified approach to causation in disparate treatment cases: Using sexual harassment by supervisors as the causal nexus for the discriminatory motivating factor in mixed motives cases." *Wisconsin Law Review* 1993:1 (January 1993), 231-259.

A unified approach to SH cases is needed according to the author. This approach shifts the burden of proof to the defendant once the plaintiff has demonstrated that the supervisor acted as harasser or condoned harassment by a co-worker, and the supervisor made an adverse employment decision. An examination of *Price Waterhouse v. Hopkins* and a discussion of a unified approach to SH are presented.

246. Kandel, William L. "Mixed motives, sexual harassment, and the Civil Rights Act of 1991." *Employee Relations Law Journal* 17:4 (Spring 1992), 635-644.

Kandel argues that the Civil Rights Act of 1991 will have a dramatic impact on the routine sexual discrimination case. Employers will lose at summary judgment cases they might have previously won, which should provide an incentive to employers to eradicate SH in the workplace.

247. Kandel, William L. "Sexual harassment: Persistent, prevalent, but preventable." *Employee Relations Law Journal* 14:3 (Winter 1988), 439-451.

After a brief review of the EEOC Guidelines, this article focuses on SH prevention programs. The author describes key elements of a prevention program, provides examples of the variety of forms a SH claim can take in the workplace, and argues for severe sanctions for violators.

248. Kennedy, Ruth A. "Insulating sexual harassment grievance procedures from the chilling effect of defamation litigation." *Washington Law Review* 69 (January 1994), 235-253.

Courts currently recognize two defenses to defamation claims arising out of an employer's SH investigation: the qualified privilege and the intracorporate immunity rule. Following an overview of the elements of defamation and the two existing defenses, Kennedy proposes a new privilege which would offer the employer a partial immunity similar to the qualified privilege, and offer the complaining employee a more complete immunity similar to the intracorporate immunity rule.

249. Kirk-Westerman, Connie, David M. Billeaux, and Robert E. England. "Ending sexual harassment at city hall: Policy initiatives in large American cities." *State and Local Government Review* 21:3 (Fall 1989), 100-105.

A survey of personnel directors in cities with populations equal to or greater than 100,000 examined municipal SH policy initiatives. The results indicated that most cities have SH policies, grievance procedures, and training programs in place. (13 refs).

250.   Konopka, Patricia A. "Combatting sexual harassment in the workplace without risking a wrongful discharge lawsuit: An employer's dilemma?" *University of Kansas Law Review* 42 (Winter 1994), 437-460.

This comment examines measures employers can take to limit their potential liability from both harassed and harassing employees. Well-publicized SH policies and comprehensive investigative procedures will protect the victim, the accused, and the employer.

251.   Koral, Alan M. "Social invitations, strict liability, and sexual harassment." *Employment Relations Today* 13:1 (Spring 1986), 13-19.

Koral discusses two court cases which he believes illustrate that even purely social invitations can constitute SH. He asserts that supervisors must be discouraged from attempting to socialize with subordinates on any basis in which a sexual connotation may be inferred.

252.   Lengnick-Hall, Mark L. "Checking out sexual harassment claims." *HRMagazine* 37:3 (March 1992), 77-81.

The author stresses that companies must follow a thorough, systematic investigative process in order to make effective decisions in SH claims. Two kinds of justice must be sought in SH investigations. One, termed procedural justice, implies that employees believe the investigative procedures to be fair. The other, termed distributive justice, implies that outcomes must be fair. Four possible investigative outcomes are discussed as are pitfalls to avoid when investigating SH complaints. (1 ref).

253.   Levy, Anne C. "The change in employer liability for supervisor sexual harassment after *Meritor*: Much ado about nothing." *Arkansas Law Review* 42:4 (Fall 1989), 795-835.

After a review of federal district and circuit courts of appeals cases, the author argues that agency principles should hold an employer to a strict standard of liability when a supervisor creates a hostile work environment.

254.   Licata, Betty Jo, and Paula M. Popovich. "Preventing sexual harassment: A proactive approach." *Training and Development Journal* 41:5 (May 1987), 34-38.

Viewing SH as a role problem that occurs when sex-role stereotypes are transferred to the workplace, the authors describe a 4-step training program that uses role negotiation techniques (RNT).

255. Oglebay, Susan, and Sue Ella Kobak. "Predicting employer liability for sexual harassment." *Employee Relations Law Journal* 12:3 (Winter 1986/1987), 412-423.

Suggesting that a supervisor's action is the area most likely to expose employers to liability for SH, the authors focus on changes in society and the workplace to alleviate the problem.

256. Oh, James J. "Internal sexual harassment complaints: Investigating to win." *Employee Relations Law Journal* 18:2 (Autumn 1992), 227-244.

This article takes the employer through the entire SH complaint investigation process. Provided are practical and legal guidelines that a company should consider before, during, and after the investigation.

257. Phillips, Michael J. "Employer sexual harassment liability under agency principles: A second look at *Meritor Savings Bank, FSB v. Vinson.*" *Vanderbilt Law Review* 44:6 (November 1991), 1229-1272.

Following an overview of *Meritor v. Vinson*, the author contends that agency law should play no role in determining employer liability for SH. An examination of this issue and recommendations are provided.

258. "Policy against sexual harassment." *Corporate Counsel's Quarterly* 7:1 (January 1991), 105-110.

As the title states, this article consists of a sample SH policy provided by Business Laws, Inc., and also includes an example of an accompanying letter used to publicize the policy.

259. Rifkind, Lawrence J., and Loretta F. Harper. "Conflict management strategies for the equal opportunity difficult person in the sexually harassing workplace." *Public Personnel Management* 23:3 (Fall 1994), 487-500.

The characteristics of sexual harassers are compared to those of the difficult personality. Many of the dysfunctional traits exhibited by difficult people, such as low self-esteem and lack of empathetic skills, are found in profiles of sexual harassers. Management strategies for coping with these individuals are offered. (37 refs).

260.   Rifkind, Lawrence J., and Loretta F. Harper. "Cross-gender immediacy behaviors and sexual harassment in the workplace: A communication paradox." *IEEE Transactions on Professional Communication* 35:4 (December 1992), 236-241.

This paper explores the paradox created by immediacy behaviors such as facial expressions, conversational topics, and disclosure. While immediacy behaviors can establish interpersonal communication and closeness among co-workers, the authors are quick to point out that gender differences in the interpretation of such behaviors can create problems related to SH. Workplace programs, it is suggested, should discuss the dimensions of SH as well as the cultural differences between men and women. (43 refs).

261.   Riger, Stephanie. "Gender dilemmas in sexual harassment policies and procedures." *American Psychologist* 46:5 (May 1991), 497-505.

Even though many companies have policies and procedures for reporting SH, the author asserts that gender bias in the policies and procedures discourages women from reporting incidents of SH. Biases in definitions and grievance procedures are examined. (83 refs).

262.   Robinson, Robert K., Billie M. Allen, Franklin Geralyn McClure, and David L. Duhon. "Sexual harassment in the workplace: A review of the legal rights and responsibilities of all parties." *Public Personnel Management* 22:1 (Spring 1993), 123-135.

After tracing the history of SH law, the authors outline the rights and responsibilities of all parties involved in SH complaints, including the employer, the charging party, and the accused. Disciplinary actions against both public and private sector employees and issues related to due process are also discussed.

263.   Ross, Cynthia S., and Robert E. England. "State governments' sexual harassment policy initiatives." *Public Administration Review* 47 (May/June 1987), 259-262.

The authors review results of a survey of state personnel directors which examined state governments' SH policy initiatives. Findings indicated that most states had SH policies in place as of 1985. An overview of Montana's state policy is included. (11 refs).

264.   Roy, Marren. "Employer liability for sexual harassment: A search for standards in the wake of *Harris v. Forklift Systems*, Inc." *SMU Law Review* 48:1 (Fall 1994), 263-294.

This article examines the judicial rulings in two SH suits: M*eritor*

Savings Bank v. Vinson and *Harris v. Forklift Systems, Inc.*
Discussed are the authors' concerns over the lack of uniform standards
for employer liability and the inconsistencies in hostile environment
SH.

265. Salsberg, Richard M. "Sexual harassment in the workplace." *Legal Administrator* 7:5 (September/October 1988), 39-44.

Salsberg provides an historical sketch of SH law. A sample SH
policy and other practical suggestions for employers are also included.

266. Sanko, Kristin D. "Employer liability and sexual harassment under
Section 1983: A comment on *Starrett v. Wadley*." *Denver University Law Review* 67:4 (Summer 1990), 571-585.

After a brief discussion of the background of Section 1983, municipal
liability for the misconduct of public officials, and the *Starrett v. Wadley* case in which the victim was denied recovery, the author
argues that a liberal approach to Section 1983 should be taken in SH
cases in order to hold municipalities liable for the unlawful activities
of their officials.

267. Smith, Bruce Chandler. "When should an employer be held liable for the
sexual harassment by a supervisor who creates a hostile work
environment? A proposed theory of liability." *Arizona State Law Journal* 19:2 (1987), 285-324.

This article discusses employer liability in hostile environment SH
claims. After a brief review of *Meritor v. Vinson*, the author presents
a theory of employer liability indicating that employers who delegate
authority to supervisors should be liable for Title VII violations
because the supervisor acts as an agent for the employer.

268. Smith, Kathleen A. "Employer liability for sexual harassment:
Inconsistency under Title VII." *Catholic University Law Review* 37:1
(Fall 1987), 245-277.

Although courts have held employers vicariously liable for
discrimination by supervisors based on race, religion, and national
origin, they have not done so for all forms of SH. The author argues
that imposing vicarious liability on employers will motivate them to
take affirmative steps to prevent workplace SH.

269. Spann, Jeri. "Dealing effectively with sexual harassment: Some practical
lessons from one city's experience." *Public Personnel Management* 19:1 (Spring 1990), 53-69.

Spann focuses on the SH policies and procedural changes made by the city government of Madison, Wisconsin. Policy and procedure development as well as workplace changes between 1979 and 1985 are discussed. (20 refs).

270. Stanley, John D. "Sexual harassment: Insight and abatement." *Business and Society* 23:1 (Spring 1984), 32-36.

This article presents a brief discussion of employer liability, characteristics of SH, and tactics to both prevent and cope with SH claims. Consensual relationships are also discussed. (11 refs).

271. Swift, Cathy Owens, and Russell L. Kent. "Selling and sales management in action- Sexual harassment: Ramifications for sales managers." *Journal of Personal Selling and Sales Management* 14:1 (Winter 1994), 77-87.

Following a brief summary of the prevalence and legal ramifications of SH in the work environment, the authors offer recommendations for sales managers. The nature of the sales profession makes the occupation prone to situations which may lead to SH. Buyer/seller relationships, complications, suggestions for handling SH complaints, and guidelines for the prevention of SH are discussed. (27 refs).

272. Tamminen, Julie M. *Sexual Harassment in the Workplace: Managing Corporate Policy.* New York: John Wiley and Sons, 1994.

This book is written for human resources personnel, unions, and others. Tamminen provides guidance on drafting and implementing preventive SH policies, developing SH training programs, handling SH charges, and addressing the scope of discovery. Several sample SH policies are included.

273. Thacker, Rebecca A. "Innovative steps to take in sexual harassment prevention." *Business Horizons* 37:1 (January/February 1994), 29-32.

Written for top management and supervisory staff, this article addresses the need for effective internal SH prevention policies and training programs. Provided are suggestions for meeting the needs of passive or compliant targets of SH, articulating the company's commitment to eliminating SH, and enforcing the company's SH prevention policy.

274. Turner, Ronald. "Employer liability under Title VII for hostile environment sexual harassment by supervisory personnel: The impact and aftermath of *Meritor Savings Bank.*" *Howard Law Journal* 33 (January 1990), 1-52.

Turner argues that, while the Meritor court clarified some aspects of SH law related to Title VII, the question of employer liability in hostile environment cases was left unanswered. Examples of employer liability rulings, before and after Meritor, are provided.

275. Wagner, Ellen J. *Sexual Harassment in the Workplace: How to Prevent, Investigate, and Resolve Problems in Your Organization*. New York, NY: AMACOM, 1992.

Given that society is becoming increasingly litigious, Wagner offers suggestions for dealing quickly and effectively with SH complaints and investigations. Discussed are the needs for proper interviewing techniques and for corroborating witnesses. The author concludes with sample investigation questions and a glossary of related legal terms.

276. Watson, Jerome R. "Employer liability for the sexually harassing actions of its customers." *Employee Relations Law Journal* 19:3 (Winter 1994), 227-237.

Over the last several years, employers have become aware that they can be held liable for the harassing actions of their employees. However, not so well known is the fact that employers can be held liable for acts of SH committed by their customers against their employees. Watson presents several practical suggestions for employers who may be faced with such claims.

277. Webb, Susan L. "Sexual harassment: Court costs rise for a persistent problem." *Management Review* 73 (December 1984), 25-28.

A six-step program for limiting employer liability in SH incidents is described and outlined. Webb recommends: determine if you have a problem, establish management support, develop a SH policy, develop complaint procedures, handle complaints, and offer training programs. Also included are future trends in SH as predicted by human rights experts.

278. Webb, Susan L. *Step Forward: Sexual Harassment in the Workplace: What You Need to Know!* New York: MasterMedia Limited, 1991.

Webb, a consultant and trainer specializing in the area of human relations, has worked with more than 60,000 employees in the area of SH since 1981. This how-to manual for managers, human resources personnel, and employees provides steps for stopping SH, educating employees, and investigating SH complaints.

8

Sexual Harassment of University Students

279. Allen, Deborah, and Judy Bessai Okawa. "A counseling center looks at sexual harassment." *Journal of the National Association for Women Deans, Administrators, and Counselors* 51:1 (Fall 1987), 9-16.

   A survey of college students explored their awareness of university SH policies and the incidence of SH at the university level. Results suggested that 12% of female respondents and 5% of male respondents had experienced at least one incident of SH. However, only 7% of female respondents correctly identified the university offices designated to handle SH complaints. (11 refs).

280. Barnett, Diane Lynne. "Sexual harassment in a university setting: The influence of respondent, victim and perpetrator characteristics." Dissertation, University of Kentucky, 1991.

281. Betts, Nancy D. "Female perceptions and evaluations of sexual harassment at Bowling Green State University (Ohio)." Dissertation, Bowling Green State University, 1984.

282. Bond, Meg A. "Division 27 sexual harassment survey: Definition, impact, and environmental context." *The Community Psychologist* 21 (1988), 7-10.

   This article describes a survey of 510 female community psychology training graduates which focused on three aspects of SH: 1) women's own SH experiences; 2) the knowledge of others' SH experiences and the impact of this on the educational environment; and 3) qualities of the graduate school environment which promote SH. Results indicate that most forms of SH appear to have a radiating impact and can affect the educational experience of all women in the program. (4 refs).

283.   Bremer, Barbara A., Cathleen T. Moore, and Ellen F. Bildersee. "Do you have to call it "sexual harassment" to feel harassed?" *College Student Journal* 25:3 (September 1991), 258-268.

In a survey of men and women at the Philadelphia College of Pharmacy and Science, the perception and labeling of SH was examined as well as knowledge of procedures for reporting SH. Six hundred eighteen faculty, staff, and students participated in this study which found significant gender differences in perception of harassing behaviors. The study also found that the female students were less likely to label situations as serious than were working women in the study. Neither group was aware of the channels for reporting SH. (19 refs).

284.   Brooks, Linda, and Annette R. Perot. "Reporting sexual harassment: Exploring a predictive model." *Psychology of Women Quarterly* 15:1 (March 1991), 31-47.

The authors discuss the development and results of their study of 490 female faculty and graduate students. This study explored the adequacy of a model for predicting the reporting of SH and the adaptation of the Sexual Experiences Questionnaire (SEQ) for collecting SH incidence data at universities. The model indicated that age, marital status, feminist ideology, and frequency of behavior would influence perceived offensiveness. Perceived offensiveness and perceived outcomes of reporting, in turn, would predict reporting behavior. The results of the study indicated that both facets have some statistical significance. (32 refs).

285.   Bursik, Krisanne. "Perceptions of sexual harassment in an academic context." *Sex Roles* 27:7/8 (October 1992), 401-412.

Bursik presents the results of her study of 124 college students which examined the influence of gender, gender role, and the power of the harasser on SH perceptions. The students evaluated vignettes which covered a range of behavioral interactions. One finding was that, in some instances, behaviors defined as SH by researchers were not viewed as SH by many of the students in this study. Also, power influenced perceptions of SH; when the harasser was a high-powered individual, the behavior was more likely to be viewed as SH. Subtle differences in the way males and females perceive behaviors are explored. (23 refs).

286. Carroll, Lynne, and Kathryn L. Ellis. "Faculty attitudes toward sexual harassment: Survey results, survey process." *Initiatives* 52:3 (Fall 1989), 35-41.

The authors report results of a study which investigated the attitudes and perceptions of 142 faculty concerning SH at a small university. Results indicated a moderate trend toward greater acceptance of SH by male faculty and that 18% of the male faculty were willing to consider that their own behavior might be perceived as sexually harassing. This article also discusses the antagonism toward this research process expressed by some members of the university community. (15 refs).

287. Cleary, Jane Scott, Claire R. Schmieler, Leona C. Parascenzo, and Nora Ambrosio. "Sexual harassment of college students: Implications for campus health promotion." *Journal of American College Health* 43:1 (July 1994), 3-10.

In a 1991 survey of 1,139 college students at Slippery Rock University, perceptions of SH and SH experiences involving faculty were examined. A 26% return rate was reported, with the findings consistent with previous studies. Eight categories of behavior were defined in the survey, with seven found to constitute SH. As many as 8% of respondents reported having experienced the three most extreme forms of SH: physical advances, explicit sexual propositions, and sexual bribery. The authors also provide policy and procedural recommendations. (33 refs).

288. Cole, Deborah Sue. "Sexual harassment in psychology training programs nationwide: Prevalence, reporting procedures and effects (grievance policy)." Dissertation, Pepperdine University, 1992.

289. Coleman, Marie M. "A study of sexual harassment of female students in academia." Dissertation, University of Wyoming, 1986.

290. Connolly, Walter B., Jr., and Alison B. Marshall. "Sexual harassment of university or college students by faculty members." *Journal of College and University Law* 15:4 (Spring 1989), 381-403.

The author examines several cases of SH in the university setting, and encourages colleges and universities to protect themselves from potential liability resulting from claims of SH. Guidelines for implementing SH policies in the university setting are presented.

291. Dietz-Uhler, Beth, and Audrey Murrell. "College students' perceptions of sexual harassment: Are gender differences decreasing?" *Journal of College Student Development* 33:6 (November 1992), 540-546.

One hundred fifty-seven college students were surveyed to identify overall attitudes toward and judgments of SH behaviors, and to determine if gender-related variables and stereotyped gender roles can predict attitudes toward SH. The authors found that males tend to be more tolerant of SH, and that both male and female students are less likely to take SH seriously when they endorse stereotypical roles of men and women. (24 refs).

292.   Dziech, Billie Wright, and Linda Weiner. *The Lecherous Professor: Sexual Harassment on Campus. 2d ed.* Urbana, IL: University of Illinois Press, 1990.

This second editions serves as a follow-up to Dziech and Weiner's 1984 landmark exploration of the SH of women students in higher education. The authors discuss the organizational, political, sexual, and social aspects of campus life that surround the issue of SH. The authors present data on the incidence and nature of SH experienced on campuses as well as offer recommendations for facilitating change.

293.   Elgart, Lloyd D., and Lillian Schanfield. "Sexual harassment of students." *Thought and Action* 7:1 (Spring 1991), 21-42.

The authors, while examining the cultural, ethical, and legal aspects of SH relevant to academic institutions, emphasize their challenge to university officials to prevent the sexual exploitation of students. Officials, they suggest, should disseminate a set of standards that protect everyone and act fairly in disciplinary procedures. (37 refs).

294.   Fairchild, Margaret Bell. "Sexual harassment and response study of female students and female faculty at the University of Southern Mississippi." Dissertation, University of Southern Mississippi, 1986.

295.   Fitzgerald, Louise F., and Alayne J. Ormerod. "Perceptions of sexual harassment: The influence of gender and academic context." *Psychology of Women Quarterly* 15:2 (June 1991), 281-294.

In a study of faculty members (163 male and 45 female) and graduate students (142 male and 172 female), 24 vignettes depicting 5 types of sexual harassment between faculty and students were presented, with social-sexual behaviors ranging from gender harassment to sexual imposition or assault. Females were significantly more likely than males to perceive less explicit situations as SH. However, uncertainty as to what constitutes SH still existed among the group studied. (20 refs).

296.   Fitzgerald, Louise F., Sandra L. Shullman, Nancy Bailey, Margaret Richards, Janice Swecker, et al. "The incidence and dimensions of

sexual harassment in academia and the workplace." *Journal of Vocational Behavior* 32:2 (April 1988), 152-175.

Because of the lack of consistent definitions of SH and an instrument to evaluate the incidence of its occurrence, the authors discuss the development, utilization, and evaluation of a standardized instrument to survey sexual harassment, the Sexual Experiences Questionnaire (SEQ). The inventory was applied to two large public universities A second form of the SEQ for working women is also described. Responses from both studies favorably assessed the results of the application of the SEQ. (29 refs).

297.   Fitzgerald, Louise F., Lauren M. Weitzman, Yael Gold, and Mimi Ormerod. "Academic harassment: Sex and denial in scholarly garb." *Psychology of Women Quarterly* 12:3 (September 1988), 329-340.

Survey responses from 235 male faculty members present a profile of social and sexual interaction between college faculty and students. Findings indicated that mentoring and friendship behaviors involving students were most frequently reported. While 26% of participants reported sexual involvement with female students, approximately 6% believed they had been sexually harassed by their female students. (11 refs).

298.   Fuhr, George Allan. "The significance of factors in judgments by Washington State Community State College faculty regarding levels of sanctions appropriate as responses to the sexual harassment of students." Dissertation, Washington State Universtiy, 1989.

299.   Gervasio, Amy Herstein, and Katy Ruckdeschel. "College students' judgments of verbal sexual harassment." *Journal of Applied Social Psychology* 22:3 (February 1992), 190-211.

The authors describe the results of their study in which 137 college students (63 women and 74 men) were asked to rate 37 sexual remarks in an attempt to differentiate verbal SH from inappropriate speech. Results revealed that subjects were more likely to rate remarks as inappropriate rather than harassing, and that female subjects found euphemisms and obscenity to be both more harassing and more inappropriate than did the male subjects. (28 refs).

300.   Glaser, Robert D., and Joseph S. Thorpe. "Unethical intimacy: A survey of sexual contact and advances between psychology educators and female graduate students." *American Psychologist* 41:1 (January 1986), 43-51.

Four hundred sixty-four female members of the Clinical Psychology Division of the American Psychological Association were surveyed concerning their experiences of sexual intimacy and sexual advances from educators during their graduate training, as well as the impact these experiences had on their professional relationships. Of the respondents, 17% indicated that sexual contact was quite prevalent, and 31% reported sexual advances which were judged by most to be overwhelmingly negative. Sexual contact between an educator and a student was considered to be unethical by most respondents. (7 refs).

301.   Gressman, George D., Claire Hamilton Usher, Sam E. Sanders, Phil L. Epstein, and Mike S. Brodowicz. "Female awareness of university sexual harassment policy." *Journal of College Student Development* 33:4 (July 1992), 370-371.

The authors report on a research project conducted to investigate the level of awareness of a university's SH policy among women in a female freshman residence hall. The project consisted of an initial survey, a 90-minute SH program, and a modified follow-up survey. Approximately one-half of respondents indicated they had experienced some form of SH. The follow-up survey indicated an increased awareness of the university SH policy and grievance procedures.

302.   Hickson, Mark III, R. D. Grierson, and Barbara C. Linder. "A communication perspective on sexual harassment: Affiliative nonverbal behaviors in asynchronous relationships." *Communication Quarterly* 39:2 (Spring 1991), 111-118.

Focusing on instructor harassment of students in higher education, the authors use a six-step process to illustrate stages in which a harasser attempts to change the nature of a relationship while the victim sends negative feedback. The authors contend that these steps could assist victims, colleagues, or administration in predicting sexually harassing behavior. (49 refs).

303.   Hoffmann, Frances L. "Sexual harassment in academia: Feminist theory and institutional practice." *Harvard Educational Review* 56:2 (May 1986), 105-121.

In an attempt to clarify the connection between social/cultural conditions and sexual harassment, the author provides a feminist critique of the problem of SH in academic institutions. She argues that SH occurs because of the disadvantaged status of women as workers and as students. By examining policies of 25 colleges and universities, she is able to point out the inconsistencies between sexual harassment theory and the formulation of guidelines. (58 refs).

304. Hotelling, Kathy. "Sexual harassment: A problem shielded by silence."
      Journal of Counseling and Development 69:6 (July/August 1991),
      497-501.

      Issues that contribute to the complexities of SH in academia are
      discussed in this article. Problems related to SH definitions, reporting
      mechanisms, victim response, prevalence data, and organizational
      climate are presented. (43 refs).

305. Hughes, Jean O'Gorman, and Berneice R. Sandler. *Peer Harassment:
      Hassles for Women on Campus.* Washington, DC: Project on the
      Status and Education of Women, 1988.

      Hughes and Sandler, writing for the Project on the Status and
      Education of Women, Association of American Colleges, focus on the
      darker side of campus life. This darker side is peer SH, specifically the
      harassment of female students by male students. The report examines
      the prevalence, impact, and causes of peer harassment. The authors
      provide five pages of recommendations for preventing and responding
      to incidents of nonsexual and SH on campuses. The report concludes
      with a list of additional publications on this and related topics
      available from the Project.

306. Hunter, Christopher, and Kent McClelland. "Honoring accounts for sexual
      harassment: A factorial survey analysis." *Sex Roles* 24:11/12 (June
      1991), 725-752.

      This study used a factorial survey analysis to examine the process of
      honoring accounts of peer SH on a college campus among students.
      Student response indicated that perceived seriousness depended on the
      reasons the perpetrator offered for his behavior, although verbal
      reactions of the victim affected perception to a lesser degree.
      Apologies and some excuses were found to reduce the perceived
      seriousness of the behavior. (50 refs).

307. Keller, Elisabeth A. "Consensual amorous relationships between faculty
      and students: The constitutional right to privacy." *Journal of College
      and University Law* 15:1 (Summer 1988), 21-42.

      Arguing that the right to form adult consensual intimate relationships
      is a fundamental freedom which must be protected, the author
      advocates the development of university policies prohibiting only
      those relationships within the instructional context together with a
      policy against SH. (14 refs).

308. Kenig, Sylvia, and John Ryan. "Sex differences in levels of tolerance and
      attribution of blame for sexual harassment on a university campus."

Sex Roles 15:9/10 (November 1986), 535-549.

A sample of university faculty, staff, and students (594 male and 715 female) were surveyed to test four hypotheses regarding sex differences and SH. As hypothesized, females were more likely than males to define behaviors as SH, males were more likely to place responsibility on the victim, females tended to disapprove of co-worker intimate relationships, and females viewed SH as a greater organizational problem than males. The authors contend that such sex differences reflect differences in perceived self-interest. Attribution theory is used to explain the sex differences. (20 refs).

309.   Little, Doric. "Sexual harassment: Faculty, student considerations." *Thought and Action* 8:1 (Spring 1992), 5-12.

Little discusses recent SH legal decisions from an academic point of view. Court rulings of particular interest to higher education personnel are summarized and recommendations are offered. (14 refs).

310.   Malovich, Natalie J. "Sexual harassment on campus: A study of students' attitudes and beliefs (victimization)." Dissertation, University of Missouri, 1985.

311.   Malovich, Natalie J., and Jayne E. Stake. "Sexual harassment on campus: Individual differences in attitudes and beliefs." *Psychology of Women Quarterly* 14:1 (March 1990), 63-81.

This study of 224 male and female college students examined the relationship between SH attitudes and two personality variables, self-esteem and sex-role attitudes. Response to scenarios and questionnaires indicated that both significantly affected attitudes toward SH. Women with high self-esteem and more traditional sex-role attitudes tended to be most tolerant of SH and least aware of its potential harm, as were males with low self-esteem. Low self-esteem women were more aware of the negative effects of SH. (23 refs).

312.   Mango, Kimberly A. "Students versus professors: Combatting sexual harassment under Title IX of the Education Amendments of 1972." *Connecticut Law Review* 23:2 (Winter 1991), 355-412.

This article traces the development of statutory rights for the student-victim of hostile environment SH in a university setting. A description of Title IX and the similarities between Title IX and Title VII are presented. The author argues that SH in education should be governed by the same judicial interpretations as SH in employment.

313. Marks, Michelle A., and Eileen S. Nelson. "Sexual harassment on campus: Effects of professor gender on perception of sexuality harassing behaviors." *Sex Roles* 28:3/4 (1993), 207-217.

     In a study of how sex of the perpetrator affects perception of SH, 35 male and 19 female undergraduates viewed 4 videotaped vignettes of student-faculty interactions in which type of behavior and gender of the harasser were manipulated. Findings revealed that incidents of blatant SH with the female as perpetrator were not perceived as less inappropriate. (20 refs).

314. Markunas, Patricia V., and Jean M. Joyce-Brady. "Underutilization of sexual harassment grievance procedures." *Journal of the National Association for Women Deans, Administrators, and Counselors* 50:3 (Spring 1987), 27-32.

     The authors report findings from their study which investigated student and employee knowledge of the illegality of SH, and the procedures to report it. Results indicated that males were more familiar with grievance procedures than females were. Those persons in higher status jobs were more familiar than those in clerical, maintenance, or security positions, and Whites knew more about procedures than minorities. (7 refs).

315. Masters, Ann Browning. "The evolution of the legal concept of environmental sexual harassment of United States higher education students by faculty." Dissertation, University of Florida, 1992.

316. McCormack, Arlene. "The sexual harassment of students by teachers: The case of students in science." *Sex Roles* 13:1/2 (July 1985), 21-32.

     Male and female students enrolled in four fields of science at 16 universities were surveyed to determine the prevalence of SH by teachers. Results indicated that 17% of the females and 2% of the males were harassed by their teachers. The results also found that females experienced an increased chance of SH as they continue their education. (30 refs).

317. McCormick, Naomi, Susan Adams-Bohley, Susan Peterson, and William Gaeddert. "Sexual harassment of students at a small college." *Initiatives* 52:3 (Fall 1989), 15-23.

     An investigation of SH of students at a small college compared how men and women, feminists and traditionalists, and faculty and students described SH problems. Surveys of 432 students and 211 faculty revealed the following: students were more likely than faculty to define social-sexual behaviors as SH; feminists defined SH more broadly than traditionalists; and that the typical sexual harasser in this study was male and either very young or at the end of mid-life. (21 refs).

318. McKinney, Kathleen. "Attitudes toward sexual harassment and perceptions of blame: Views of male and female graduate students." *Free Inquiry in Creative Sociology* 18:1 (May 1990), 73-76.

A mail survey of 281 male and female graduate students explored their attitudes and attributions of blame for incidents of faculty-student SH. Results indicate that while both males and females attribute greater blame for SH to external factors such as the faculty member, females did so to a greater degree. (25 refs).

319. McKinney, Kathleen, Carol Voiles Olson, and Arthur Satterfield. "Graduate students' experiences with and responses to sexual harassment: A research note." *Journal of Interpersonal Violence* 3:3 (September 1988), 319-325.

A survey of 281 graduate students (132 males and 149 females) investigating their experiences with and responses to SH by faculty while in graduate schools indicated that 9% of male and 35% of female subjects reported they had been sexually harassed. The authors argue that power in the student-teacher relationships was evident as the SH was more likely delivered by professors than by lecturers or instructors. (12 refs).

320. Mitchell, Susan Elizabeth. "Creating campus climates that are free from sexual harassment: Implications for leaders in higher education." Dissertation, University of San Diego, 1994.

321. Murrell, Audrey J., and Beth L. Dietz-Uhler. "Gender identity and adversarial sexual beliefs as predictors of attitudes toward sexual harassment." *Psychology of Women Quarterly* 17:2 (June 1993), 169-175.

One hundred seven college students (52 female and 55 males) participated in this study which examined whether personal orientation, SH experience, gender identity, and adversarial sexual beliefs can predict attitudes toward SH among college students. Direct experience with SH predicted negative attitudes (less tolerant) toward SH for males while gender identity predicted negative attitudes toward SH for females. (12 refs).

322. Olson, Carol, and Kathleen McKinney. "Processes inhibiting the reduction of sexual harassment in academe: An alternative

explanation." *Initiatives* 52:3 (Fall 1990), 7-13.

The authors argue that the persistence of SH on university campuses is explained by two dramas taking place simultaneously: the dynamics between student and harasser, and the dynamics involving the organizational administration. Exploration of patterns of social interaction which prevail in SH is recommended. (15 refs).

323. Padgitt, Steven C., and Janet S. Padgitt. "Cognitive structure of sexual harassment: Implications for university policy." *Journal of College Student Personnel* 27:1 (January 1986), 34-39.

Three hundred seventy-three college students were surveyed to determine their ability to distinguish between sexually harassing and offensive behavior, and how these behaviors might be organized along a continuum. Results indicated that women subjects were able to clearly distinguish between the two types of behaviors and viewed harassing behavior as offensive. Male subjects, however, sometimes answered that harassing behavior was not offensive. The continuum for sexually harassing behaviors was not fully supported, indicating a need for further research in this area. (16 refs).

324. Paludi, Michele A., ed. *Ivory Power: Sexual Harassment on Campus.* Albany, NY: State University of New York Press, 1990.

This edited book encompasses a wide variety of SH issues facing university administrators, faculty, and students today, including program development and SH prevention, federal laws, student victimization, racism, student-teacher relationships, and teacher harassment of students. The contributing authors have all conducted research, developed policies, or conducted training session on SH or related forms of victimization. Sample workshop materials are included in the appendices.

325. Paludi, Michele A., and Darlene C. DeFour. "Research on sexual harassment in the academy: Definitions, findings, constraints, responses." *Initiatives* 52:3 (Fall 1989), 43-49.

This article reviews SH literature concerning the definition of SH, incidence, and profiles of harassers. The authors point out generalizations included in previous research, and discuss the use of previous research results in educational training programs offered today. (36 refs).

326. Pickrell, Juliana Evan Holway. "Academic sexual harassment: Sexual

harassment of students." Dissertation, University of Washington, 1986.

327. Popovich, Paula M., Betty Jo Licata, Deeann Nokovich, Theresa Martelli, and Sheryl Zoloty. "Assessing the incidence and perceptions of sexual harassment behaviors among American undergraduates." *Journal of Psychology* 120:4 (July 1986), 387-396.

Two studies of male and female college students with job experience were conducted to develop a 9-item scale of SH behaviors, assess the incidence of these behaviors, determine the degree to which the behaviors are considered SH, and why. Findings indicated the importance of considering the position of the harasser in assessing perceptions of SH. (7 refs).

328. Reilly, Mary Ellen, Bernice Lott, and Sheila M. Gallogly. "Sexual harassment of university students." *Sex Roles* 15:7/8 (October 1986), 333-358.

The SH experiences of 393 undergraduate and graduate students were studied to determine SH incidence in the classroom, outside the classroom, and on the job. Attitudes toward harassing behaviors were measured by the Tolerance for Sexual Harassment Inventory (TSHI). Men were found to be more tolerant of SH than women, as were young students in general. (25 refs).

329. Reilly, Mary Ellen, Bernice Lott, Donna Caldwell, and Luisa DeLuca. "Tolerance for sexual harassment related to self-reported sexual victimization." *Gender and Society* 6:1 (March 1992), 122-138.

The authors outline results of a study of 920 students (534 females and 386 males) from the University of Rhode Island which examined individual differences among men and women with respect to self-reported beliefs and behaviors relevant to SH and victimization. Of the results, men were more tolerant of sexually harassing behaviors, more likely to believe heterosexual relationships are adversarial, more likely to believe rape myths, and more likely to admit they might sexually assault someone. (37 refs).

330. Roscoe, Bruce, Megan P. Goodwin, Susan E. Repp, and Marshall Rose. "Sexual harassment of university students and student-employees: Findings and implications." *College Student Journal* 21:3 (Fall 1987), 254-273.

A random sample of students (366 females and 139 males) at Central Michigan University were surveyed on sexually harassing behaviors they had experienced as students or as student employees, identification of perpetrators, circumstances under which SH occurred, and response to SH. Findings indicate that 28% of female students and 12% of male students had experienced some form of SH but only 8% of the females and 6% of the males identified the behaviors as SH. Implications for university administrators and professionals who work with students are discussed. (27 refs).

331.　Rubin, Linda J., and Sherry B. Borgers. "Sexual harassment in universities during the 1980's." *Sex Roles* 23:7/8 (October 1990), 397-411.

Rubin and Borgers present an overview of 20 research studies published since 1980 concerning faculty-student SH in higher education. The need for a commonly accepted definition of SH and a standardized research instrument are emphasized. (23 refs).

332.　Ryan, John, and Sylvia Kenig. "Risk and ideology in sexual harassment." *Sociological Inquiry* 61:2 (Spring 1991), 231-241.

The authors report results of their SH study involving a sample of university faculty, staff, and students which suggested that little statistical variation exists between the report of SH and risk factors such as organizational position, demographic characteristics, and gender-role ideology. (14 refs).

333.　Schneider, Beth E. "Graduate women, sexual harassment, and university policy." *Journal of Higher Education* 58:1 (January/February 1987), 46-65.

Schneider describes the results of a survey of 356 graduate women which found that 60% of respondents had experienced at least one form of "everyday harassment" by male faculty during their studies. Thirteen percent of respondents reported having consensually dated a faculty member at least once, while 9% reported coercive dating or coercive sexual incidents. Proposals for SH prevention include a clearly defined policy, educational training programs for both students and faculty, and penalties for offenders. (49 refs).

334.　Scott, Deborah Deprez. "Sexual harassment behaviors, management strategies, and power-dependence relationships among a female graduate student population." Dissertation, Ball State University, 1984.

335.　Singer, Terry L. "Sexual harassment in graduate schools of social work: Provocative dilemmas." *Journal of Social Work Education* 25:1 (Winter 1989), 68-76.

Singer summarizes the results of a 1987 survey of deans and directors of schools of social work. This survey explored the nature and incidence of SH within social work programs. Findings revealed that over half of all programs had reports of SH over the five year period examined. Characteristics of both victims and perpetrators of SH are included.

336. Small, Mary Jo. "The guardians of Heloise? Sexual harassment in higher education." *Educational Record* 70:2 (Spring 1989), 42-45.

Small asserts that, if an academic institution's primary purpose is to create an environment in which teaching and research can be successfully pursued, then SH negatively impacts the heart of its mission. From this, the author reviews such issues as consensual relationships, freedom of speech, humor, and effective enforcement of SH policies.

337. Stockdale, Margaret S., and Alan Vaux. "What sexual harassment experiences lead respondents to acknowledge being sexually harassed? A secondary analysis of a university survey." *Journal of Vocational Behavior* 43:2 (October 1993), 221-234.

A sample of 310 university faculty and staff, 822 undergraduates and 227 graduate students were surveyed to determine what kinds of experiences lead men and women to state they have been sexually harassed. Results indicated that experiencing sexual seduction, sexual coercion, and sexual imposition increased the odds of SH acknowledgment. (29 refs).

338. Struckman-Johnson, Cindy, and David Struckman-Johnson. "College men's and women's reactions to hypothetical sexual touch varied by initiator gender and coercion level." *Sex Roles* 29:5/6 (September 1993), 371-385.

152 male and 152 female heterosexual college students read a vignette in which they were to imagine receiving an uninvited genital touch, either gentle or forceful, from either a classmate of the opposite or same sex. The female students had strong negative reactions from both opposite or same sex touch, whether gentle or forceful. Men received negative reactions from other males. Women's reactions to same-sex touch were found to be more related to anti-homosexual feelings than were men's. (25 refs).

339. Sullivan, Mary. "Sexual harassment of university students: Students' perceptions and responses." Dissertation, Michigan State University, 1985.

340. Sullivan, Mary, and Deborah I. Bybee. "Female students and sexual harassment: What factors predict reporting behavior?" *Journal of the National Association for Women Deans, Administrators, and Counselors* 50:2 (Winter 1987), 11-16.

This study of 219 college women examined the predictors of reporting SH incidents and the effects of the severity of the harassment on reporting behavior. Results showed that reporting behavior was affected by four factors: 1) the severity of the SH; 2) fear of the reporting procedures; 3) the perceived effectiveness of reporting; and 4) concern for being believed. (12 refs).

341. Sundt, Melora Ann. "Identifying the attitudes and beliefs that accompany sexual harassment." Dissertation, University of California, Los Angeles, 1994.

342. Tuana, Nancy. "Sexual harassment in academe: Issues of power and coercion." *College Teaching* 33:2 (Spring 1985), 53-63.

The relationship of SH to power and coercion in academic settings is examined. Using five categories of SH activity, the author develops a conceptual analysis of sexual behavior. She demonstrates coercive actions in each category which have a negative impact upon the educational environment. (24 refs).

343. Virella, Basilisa. "Incidence, perceptions and attitudes toward sexual harassment in higher education." Dissertation, University of Wisconsin, 1989.

344. Weil, Marie, Michelle Hughes, and Nancy Hooyman, eds. *Sexual Harassment and Schools of Social Work: Issues, Costs, and Strategic Responses*. Alexandria, VA: Council on Social Work Education, Inc., 1994.

The authors of this work range from experienced speakers on the subject of SH in schools of social work to emerging scholars. Educational initiatives and practical suggestions are provided for the prevention of SH in schools of social work, as well as ways to deal with it when SH occurs. The appendices include sample policies for classroom and field settings and educational training materials.

9

Sexual Harassment of University Faculty and Staff

345. Bandy, Nancy Lee. "Sexual harassment of female employees at a midwestern university." Dissertation, Southern Illinois University, 1989.

346. Benson, Katherine A. "Comment on Crocker's 'An analysis of university definitions of sexual harassment.'" *Signs: Journal of Women in Culture and Society* 9:3 (Spring 1984), 516-519.

    The author extends the definition of SH offered by Crocker to include cases of contrapower harassment. She defines contrapower sexual harassment as SH in which the victim has formal power over the abuser and cites examples of SH of women professors by their male students. (3 refs).

347. Fouad, Nadya A., and Robert T. Carter. "Gender and racial issues for new counseling psychologists in academia." *Counseling Psychologist* 20:1 (January 1992), 123-140.

    This article focuses on the coping skills of women and racial/ethnic group members beginning their academic counseling careers. The authors contend that responding appropriately to SH is a critical competency for new female professors. Recommendations are offered both for the new professional and the academic units that hire them. (31 refs).

348. Goodwin, Megan P., Bruce Roscoe, Marshall Rose, and Susan E. Repp. "Sexual harassment: Experiences of university employees." *Initiatives* 52:3 (Fall 1989), 25-33.

    Four hundred forty-nine employees were surveyed at Central Michigan

University (CMU) to determine the extent to which they had experienced SH in the workplace. Thirty-nine percent of the female respondents and 19% of the males reported experiencing some form of SH at CMU. The harassing behaviors cited most frequently by males and females were sexist behaviors, comments, and body language. The most frequently cited perpetrator for both male and female respondents was a male coworker. (24 refs).

349.   Grauerholz, Elizabeth. "Sexual harassment of women professors by students: Exploring the dynamics of power, authority, and gender in a university setting." *Sex Roles* 21:11/12 (December 1989), 789-801.

This study examined the SH of female professors by students. The 208 women who participated in this study reported a variety of behaviors ranging from sexist comments to sexual assault and used avoidance or confrontation to deal with the minor instances of SH. A discussion of contrapower SH and gender roles is included. (20 refs).

350.   McKinney, Kathleen. "Contrapower sexual harassment: The effects of student sex and type of behavior on faculty perceptions." *Sex Roles* 27:11/12 (December 1992), 627-643.

In this study, 375 male and female faculty at two Illinois universities were asked to read a vignette about a situation between an opposite sex student and a faculty member. They then made judgments as to whether that event constituted sexual harassment. The findings reveal that the gender of the student offender as well as the type of behavior influenced perceptions of the behavior. Both male and female subjects saw the incident as more problematic when the victim was female. In addition, female subjects were more likely to view the behavior as sexual harassment, to think the faculty member would be more upset, and to hold the student more responsible than male subjects. Role theory is utilized to provide a theoretical framework for analysis. (25 refs).

351.   McKinney, Kathleen. "Sexual harassment of university faculty by colleagues and students." *Sex Roles* 23:7/8 (October 1990), 421-438.

This study of 188 university faculty investigated faculty as victims of SH by both colleagues and students. Women faculty reported more incidents of SH by colleagues than by students while men reported more SH by students. Incidents of SH were most often not formally reported by respondents in this study. (45 refs).

352.   McKinney, Kathleen. "Sexual harassment and college faculty members." *Deviant Behavior* 15:2 (April/June 1994), 171-191.

Unlike most SH studies which rely on survey questionnaires or experiments, the study described here involved open-ended exploratory interviews of 10 male and 17 female college faculty. Each faculty member had some experience as a victim, an offender, or an accused party in at least one SH incident involving a student or colleague. While respondents acknowledged the subjective nature of SH, most of their SH definitions matched the legal forms of quid pro quo and hostile environment SH. (34 refs).

353. McKinney, Kathleen, and Kelly Crittenden. "Contrapower sexual harassment: The offender's viewpoint." *Free Inquiry in Creative Sociology* 20:1 (May 1992), 3-10.

This article discusses the results of a survey of 155 undergraduates (52 male and 103 female) as to the nature and prevalence of SH of professors by students. While none of the students admitted harassing professors, the data suggested that 18% of participants engaged in behaviors that faculty find harassing. Reasons for these behaviors and gender differences in attitudes are also discussed. (25 refs).

354. Sandler, Bernice Resnick. "Women faculty at work in the classroom, or, why it still hurts to be a woman in labor." *Communication Education* 40:1 (January 1991), 6-15.

This essay examines the different ways in which male and female students communicate with male and female faculty. Several examples are used to illustrate how female faculty are often viewed as less competent, harassed by male students, and generally devalued. The author provides suggestions for actively dealing with inappropriate student behaviors. (19 refs).

355. Yates, William Tennyson , II. "An examination of sexual harassment in the academic workplace." Dissertation, Saint Louis University, 1987.

10

Sexual Harassment of Elementary and High School Students

356. Bogart, Karen, and Nan Stein. "Breaking the silence: Sexual harassment in education." *Peabody Journal of Education* 64:4 (Summer 1987), 146-163.

   Based on surveys and interviews conducted by the Massachusetts Department of Education and the Carnegie Corporation of New York, Bogart and Stein present an overview of SH issues in education. The focus is on both high school and college levels. Problems such as teacher-student SH and student-student SH are discussed, as are strategies for preventing SH situations. (32 refs).

357. Corbett, Kelly, Cynthia S. Gentry, and Willie Pearson, Jr. "Sexual harassment in high school." *Youth and Society* 25:1 (September 1993), 93-103.

   In a survey of 185 undergraduates (49% female), students were asked to recall instances of their own SH experiences in high school as well as those of other students. While they did not think SH was a serious problem, 6% reported experiencing SH and half reported incidents involving other students. Over one-third knew of sexual relationships between teachers and students, although the majority felt that the relationships were consensual in nature. The authors speculate that high school students lack the experience to recognize and name certain experiences as SH. (20 refs).

358. Davis, Karen Mellencamp. "Reading, writing, and sexual harassment: Finding a constitutional remedy when schools fail to address peer abuse." *Indiana Law Journal* 69:4 (Fall 1994), 1123-1163.

Davis points out that legislation or litigation has been necessary to prompt schools to address the growing problem of student-student SH. Discussed are routes for students to take when seeking to hold schools responsible for SH inflicted by other students. Possible opportunities under Due Process and Equal Protection Clauses or Title VII exist.

359. Decker, Robert H. "Eleven ways to stamp out the potential for sexual harassment." *American School Board Journal* 175:8 (August 1988), 28-29, 38.

The author contends that, as the official employer in a school system, board members should be prepared to handle SH cases. Eleven steps to assist school officials in handling SH complaints and sample SH policy are presented.

360. Dolan, Helena K. "The fourth R- Respect: Combatting peer sexual harassment in the public schools." *Fordham Law Review* 63:1 (October 1994), 215-244.

Dolan presents a detailed examination of peer SH in America's schools. The pervasiveness of the problem is discussed, including the 1993 American Association of University Women (AAUW) survey of high school students which revealed that 85% of girls and 76% of boys reported unwelcome sexual behavior. Arguing that students have a constitutional right to affirmative state protection in public schools, the author proposes a model for action against peer SH.

361. Getty, Wendy Gomez. "Sexual harassment and the public school." *School Business Affairs* 59:7 (July 1993), 44-46.

Getty examines the effect of Title IX on the SH of high school students and the impact of the *Franklin v. Gwinnett County Public Schools* decision on the responses of school districts to complaints of SH. In *Franklin*, the court determined that where a private cause of action exists, monetary damages from school districts and individuals must also exist. Strategies school districts can use to prevent SH and avoid liability are offered.

362. Lackey, Donald. "Sexual harassment in sports." *Physical Educator* 47:2 (1990), 22-26.

This article explores the SH of high school female athletes by male coaches. Female participants of athletics in college and former participants of high school athletics (n=264) from several colleges were surveyed about incidents of SH, including profanity, fondling, and intercourse. Although findings showed there were cited forms of

SH, 88% of respondents reported that SH was not a problem at their school. (2 refs).

363. LeClair, Laurie. "Sexual harassment between peers under Title VII and Title IX: Why girls just can't wait to be working women." *Vermont Law Review* 16:1 (Summer 1991), 303-339.

      LeClair focuses on SH between adolescent students in this article. She proposes expanding Title IX to protect students from a sexually derogatory environment just as Title VII protects working women.

364. Rosen, Barbara Ann. "Sexual harassment of high school females: Its relation to race/ethnicity, socioeconomic status, and school charasteristics." Dissertation, Rutgers, the State University of New Jersey, 1994.

365. Sherer, Monica L. "No longer just child's play: School liability under Title IX for peer sexual harassment." *University of Pennsylvania Law Review* 141:5 (May 1993), 2119-2168.

      Student-to-student SH in elementary and secondary school settings is the subject of this article. The consequences of peer SH and a proposal to expand Title IX to the public school environment are discussed.

366. Stein, Nan D., and Lisa Sjostrom. *Flirting or Hurting: A Teacher's Guide on Student-to-Student Sexual Harassment in Schools (Grades 6 Through 12)*. Washington, DC: National Educational Association, 1994.

      The authors provide a teaching guide aimed at raising student awareness about SH and opening discussions of related topics. Reading, writing, discussion, and role playing assignments are included. Suggestions for ways to incorporate the materials into the classroom as well as how to involve parents are provided.

367. Strauss, JoAnn. "Peer sexual harassment of high school students: A reasonable student standard and an affirmative duty imposed on educational institutions." *Law and Inequality: A Journal of Theory and Practice* 10:2/3 (Winter 1992), 163-186.

      SH litigation at the high school level is examined. The author proposes a "reasonable student" standard for peer SH and advocates training to educate students about SH while they are in high school.

368. Strauss, Susan. "Sexual harassment in the school: Legal implications for principals." *NASSP Bulletin* 72:506 (March 1988), 93-97.

Strauss reports findings of a study of high school juniors and seniors of the prevalence of SH, coping techniques, and feelings about the SH. Results indicated that SH is widespread, with teachers representing nearly 30% of the perpetrators. Differences between SH and flirtation are discussed as are SH prevention strategies.

369.   Wishnietsky, Dan H. "Reported and unreported teacher-student sexual harassment." *Journal of Educational Research* 84:3 (January/February 1991), 164-169.

Sixty-five North Carolina school superintendents and 148 high school seniors were surveyed to determine the extent of SH between teachers and students, the duration of the relationships, and any disciplinary action taken. Results indicated a significant discrepancy between the number of SH incidents reported by superintendents and the number reported by students. Recommendations for the prevention of SH are offered. (13 refs).

370.   Wishnietsky, Dan, and Dennis Felder. "Assessing coach-student relationships." *Journal of Physical Education, Recreation and Dance* 60:7 (September 1989), 76-79.

The authors discuss results of their survey of school superintendents in North Carolina which investigated the frequency of and discipline for improper relationships between coaches and students. Nineteen incidents of improper conduct were reported. Legal recommendations for school systems and students are also included. (9 refs).

11

Institutional Responsibility: Preventive and Corrective Actions at School

371. American Association of University Professors. "Sexual harassment:
      Suggested policy and procedures for handling complaints." in *AAUP
      Policy Documents and Reports*, Washington, D.C.: American
      Association of University Professors, 1990, 113-115.

      This report, adopted as AAUP policy in June 1990, proposes a
      statement of policy and applicable procedures for filing and resolving
      SH complaints in university settings.

372. Beauvais, Kathleen. "Workshops to combat sexual harassment: A case
      study of changing attitudes." *Signs: Journal of Women in Culture and
      Society* 12:1 (Fall 1986), 130-145.

      In a study of 53 residence hall staff at the University of Michigan, the
      effectiveness of the "Tell Someone" SH training program was
      explored. Pre- and post-workshop surveys were conducted to determine
      how participants' attitudes toward and knowledge of SH changed due to
      this workshop. The author found the training program to be a
      successful intervention in combating SH. Recommendations for
      further research in this area are included.

373. Clair, Robin P. "The bureaucratization, commodification, and
      privatization of sexual harassment through institutional discourse."
      Management Communication Quarterly 7:2 (November 1993), 123-
      157.

      Nine of eleven Big Ten universities participated in the author's
      analysis of their SH policies, guidelines, and brochures. The author
      suggests that three forms of discourse contribute to the patriarchal
      practices of bureaucratization, commodification, and privatization of

SH: 1) taken-for-granted discourse; 2) strategic ambiguity; and 3) exclusionary discourse. (101 refs).

374.   Cole, Elsa Kircher. "Recent legal developments in sexual harassment." *Journal of College and University Law* 13:3 (Winter 1986), 267-284.

This article applies recent developments in SH law to institutions of higher education. Cole suggests that, in light of *Meritor*, supervisors, faculty, and students should be educated about the more subtle forms of SH as well as the obvious forms of quid pro quo harassment. Issues related to damages and disciplinary action are discussed.

375.   Czapanskiy, Karen. "Anti-harassment: Building law school policies." *Maryland Journal of Contemporary Legal Issues* 4:2 (Spring/Summer 1993), 163-170.

Czapanskiy, past Chair of the Section on Women in Legal Education, reports the results of the committee's recent efforts to develop a comprehensive set of principles for combating SH in law schools. Those principles agreed upon include a definition of SH which includes those groups who have historically suffered, and educational efforts taken for both prophylactic reasons and in response to particular incidents.

376.   Didgna, Thomas F. "The development and implementation of an educational program relative to sexual victimization." Dissertation, University of Florida, 1985.

377.   Divisek, Faith McCall. "Sexual harassment policies in public school disctricts in New Jersey: Implications for educational administration." Dissertation, Columbia University Teachers College, 1994.

378.   Fortunato, Ray T. "Guideline for policy on sexual harassment," in *A Handbook for Developing Higher Education Personnel Policies*, Washington, D.C.: College and University Personnel Association, 1988, 314-324.

Developed to assist personnel officers in writing policies, the SH policy outlined in this manual presents several aspects of policy wording and implementation. Informal and formal disciplinary measures are suggested.

379.   Gehlauf, Deeann Nokovich. "Supervisory responses to incidents of sexual harassment: The effect of managerial and situational factors." Dissertation, Ohio University, 1989.

380. Gustafson, Thomas James. "Sexual harassment: The faculty context at a comprehensive public university." Dissertation, University of Vermont, 1991.

381. Harper, Loretta F., and Lawrence J. Rifkind. "Competent communication strategies for responding to sexual harassment in colleges and universities." *CUPA Journal* 43:2 (Summer 1992), 33-40.

As the workplace becomes increasingly diverse, the need to understand the verbal and non-verbal behavioral differences between men and women becomes critical. The authors review the literature concerning gender and communication styles, gender and power, and gender roles, and include suggestions for developing strategies to respond to SH in colleges and universities. (35 refs).

382. Hayward, Peggy Freer. "Survey and analysis of sexual harassment policies and procedures and educational programs affecting students in the California State University." Dissertation, University of Southern California, 1989.

383. Howard, Sharon. "Organizational resources for addressing sexual harassment." *Journal of Counseling and Development* 69:6 (July/August 1991), 507-511.

The author stresses the importance of effective SH policies and complaint procedures in academic institutions. Sexual harassment prevention programs need to include both the widespread dissemination of SH policies and education programs for those most likely to receive complaints of SH. (29 refs).

384. Keller, Elisabeth A. "Consensual relationships and institutional policy." *Academe* 76:1 (January/February 1990), 29-32.

Arguing that the right to form adult consensual intimate relationships is a fundamental freedom which must be protected, the author advocates the development of university policies prohibiting only those relationships within the instructional context and a policy against SH. (14 refs).

385. Kohl, John P., and Paul S. Greenlaw. "The who, what, and when of sexual harassment: Teaching tips for business educators." *Journal of Education for Business* 68:6 (July 1993), 358.

Kohl and Greenlaw trace the history of workplace SH, paying particular attention to landmark court decisions. Suggestions for incorporating such information into management and personnel courses are offered. In order not to wear out the topic, they urge departments to coordinate their efforts. The authors feel that instructors have an unparalleled opportunity to teach future managers about their obligations under the law. (6 refs).

386. Kors, Alan Charles. "Harassment policies in the university." *Society* 28:4 (May/June 1991), 22-30.

Kors challenges his readers to be open minded when considering implications of the "harassment" issue at universities. He argues that SH policies in academia raise serious problems, particularly regarding the First Amendment Right of Free Speech.

387. Lewis, John F., and Susan C. Hastings. *Sexual Harassment in Education, 2d ed.* Topeka, KS: National Organization on Legal Problems of Education, 1994.

The authors examine the legal and institutional implications of SH in an academic institution, focusing on specific aspects of institutional liability for SH of employees and students. These aspects include: romance and harassment, the duty to protect, negligent hiring, the duty to warn, and publicity and insurance concerns. The appendixes include checklists for prevention of liability and conducting investigations, and a sample SH policy.

388. Little, Doric Alison. "An investigation of the legal parameters of policies dealing with sexual relationships in academe." Dissertation, Unversity of Hawaii, 1987.

389. Little, Doric, and John A. Thompson. "Campus policies, the law and sexual relationships." *Thought and Action* 5:1 (Spring 1989), 17-24.

Following a summarization of key SH cases, the authors report the results of their recent study of existing SH policies or codes of ethics at a random sample of colleges and universities; 32 were found to have SH policies. A guide for the development of policies dealing with sexual relationships in academia is appended. (20 refs).

390. Lott, Bernice. "Sexual harassment: Consequences and remedies." *Thought and Action* 8:2 (Winter 1993), 89-104.

Lott argues that there continues to be much resistance to the subject of SH by both men and women in academia. Following a review of studies concerning the tolerance of SH, Lott recommends educational programs to help reduce the incidence of other hostile behaviors directed toward women. (18 refs).

391. Murcar, Marguerite Joanne. "A study of the effects of policy and type of institutions on the sexual harassment of students in institutions of higher education in the state of Washington." Dissertation, Gonzaga University, 1988.

392. Olswang, Steven G. "Reassessing effective procedures in cases of sexual harassment." *New Directions for Institutional Research* 19:76 (Winter 1992), 49-56.

Olswang, vice provost and professor in the College of Education at the University of Washington, Seattle, provides a case example of an institutional response to the SH of students by faculty. The case illustrates the obsolescence of faculty-only collegial reviews where a faculty member's job is at stake. In many circumstances involving SH, victims, whether students or staff, are demanding participation in the dispute resolution process. (9 refs).

393. Paludi, Michele A. "Creating new taboos in the academy: Faculty responsibility in preventing sexual harassment." *Initiatives* 52:4 (Winter 1990), 29-34.

Paludi argues that faculty need to assume responsibility for creating colleges free of SH. She re-examines research which looks at faculty perceptions of SH and the power faculty members have over students. Several SH educational training programs implemented at Hunter College are also discussed. (19 refs).

394. Paludi, Michele A. "Ethnicity, sex, and sexual harassment." *Thought and Action* 8:2 (Winter 1993), 105-116.

Paludi addresses the impact of SH in academic institutions, with particular emphasis on the SH of ethnic minority women. Recommendations for educational programs and complaint procedures are offered. (24 refs).

395. Paludi, Michele A., and Richard B. Barickman. *Academic and Workplace Sexual Harassment: A Resource Manual.* Albany, NY: State University of New York Press, 1991.

The authors, lecturers and consultants on academic SH, provide an overview of academic and workplace SH definitions and incidence. Methods for preventing SH complaints are also suggested. Related articles on academic and workplace SH are included in the appendices.

396. Penn, Michaele Paulette. "An investigation of sexual harassment provisions in Virginia school district policy." Dissertation, Virginia Polytechnic Institute and State University, 1989.

397. Rhodes, Frank H. T. "The moral imperative to prevent sexual harassment on campus." *Initiatives* 52:4 (Winter 1990), 1-4.

      Rhodes emphasizes the prevalence of SH on university campuses and discusses harassing behaviors that stem from power relationships and harassing behaviors among peers. Examples of educational techniques used to combat SH at Cornell University are provided.

398. Robertson, Claire, Constance E. Dyer, and D'Ann Campbell. "Campus harassment: Sexual harassment policies and procedures at institutions of higher learning." *Signs: Journal of Women in Culture and Society* 13:4 (Summer 1988), 792-812.

      The authors discuss the results of a survey of 311 public and private colleges and universities concerning their SH policies and procedures. The survey covered three points: the content of SH policies and procedures, methods of handling SH complaints, and assessments of the effectiveness of policies and procedures. Results indicated that public schools were much more likely to have SH policies and procedures than were private schools, few sanctions were imposed at any of the schools, and most complaints were handled informally. Recommendations based on this survey are presented.

399. Schneider, Ronna Greff. "Sexual harassment and higher education." *Texas Law Review* 65:3 (February 1987), 525-583.

      SH in the educational setting is the focus of this article. Relief under Title IX and Title VII is examined as are the problems of institutional liability and grievance procedures.

400. Shoop, Robert J., and Debra L. Edwards. *How to Stop Sexual Harassment in Our Schools: A Handbook and Curriculum Guide for Administrators and Teachers.* Boston: Allyn and Bacon, 1994.

      Shoop, a professor of educational law, and Edwards, an elementary school principal, argue that students must learn appropriate behavior very early in life if SH is to be eradicated. This book discusses the legal and educational aspects of SH in elementary and secondary schools. Detailed curriculum guides for grades K-12 as well as sample district SH policies and complaint procedures are included.

401. Sullivan, George M. "Employer liability for sexual harassment extends to schools and universities." *Labor Law Journal* 43:7 (July 1992), 456-461.

      With the case of *Franklin v. Gwinnett County Public Schools*, the

Supreme Court for the first time included universities and schools among employers who could be held liable for money damages for SH of employees or, as in this case, students.

402. Thomann, Daniel A., Donald E. Strickland, and Judith L. Gibbons. "An organizational development approach to preventing sexual harassment: Developing shared commitment through awareness training." *CUPA Journal* 40:3 (Fall 1989), 34-43.

Stressing the importance of going beyond SH policy distribution, the authors describe the development and structure of the SH training program at St. Louis University. Designed by an external consultant using a client-centered approach, this program aims to establish shared meaning and a common understanding of the human toll and instructional implications of SH. (45 refs).

403. Truax, Anne. "Sexual harassment in higher education: What we've learned." *Thought and Action* 5:1 (Spring 1989), 25-38.

Twelve years at the Minnesota Women's Center provides the author with the foundation for this article. SH issues pertinent to college and university personnel are reviewed and an annotated bibliography and fact sheet are appended.

404. Wagner, K. C. "Prevention and intervention: Developing campus policy and procedures." *Initiatives* 52:4 (Winter 1990), 37-45.

Wagner, past Director of the Working Women's Institute and expert witness in SH hearings, discusses the necessary components of successful SH policies and complaint procedures. To be credible, policies must meet three goals: prevent SH, remedy SH situations, and properly punish perpetrators. Excerpts from actual university policies are provided. (14 refs).

405. West, Ellen L., Candyce Reynolds, and Janice Jackson. "Addressing sexual harassment: A strategy for changing the climate in higher education." *NASPA Journal* 31:2 (Winter 1994), 130-136.

The authors, all from Portland State University (PSU), argue that the existence of laws prohibiting SH and the development of complaint procedures will not alone insure that complaints are brought or that campus SH will decline. Because of the need for the development of new and creative methods for dealing with campus SH, the PSU Sexual Harassment Resource Network was created. This network provides students with an informal group of faculty and staff they can contact regarding SH. (19 refs).

406.   Wetherby, Ivor Lois. "Policies and grievance procedures regarding sexual harassment in Florida community colleges: An examination, evaluation, and comparison with court decisions." Dissertation, Florida International University, 1992.

12

Sexual Harassment of Women of Color, Lesbians, Gay Men, and Bisexuals

407. Crenshaw, Kimberle. "Race, gender, and sexual harassment." *Southern California Law Review* 65:3 (March 1992), 1467-1476.

    This paper, based on a speech given at a 1991 Forum for Women State Legislators, explores the SH of Black women. Stereotypes about Black women are presented as are methods for dispelling such misconceptions.

408. D'Augelli, Anthony R. "Lesbians' and gay men's experiences of discrimination and harassment in a university community." *American Journal of Community Psychology* 17:3 (June 1989), 317-321.

    This article describes a study at Pennsylvania State University which investigated the incidence of discrimination, harassment, and violence among 125 lesbians and gay men. The author found that gay men were victimized more than lesbian women, and that fear for personal safety was experienced by 64% of respondents. However, incidents were rarely reported to authorities. Suggestions for victim support are included. (8 refs).

409. Johnson, Linda Joyce. "The effect of sexual harassment against black women in the work place." Dissertation, California State University, Fullerton, 1992.

410. Norris, Megan P., and Mark A. Randon. "Sexual orientation and the workplace: Recent developments in discrimination and harassment law." *Employee Relations Law Journal* 19:2 (Autumn 1993), 233-246.

This article compares those cases involving homosexual sexual advances to those cases of heterosexual sexual advances. Homosexual advances, the authors point out, may give rise to either quid pro quo or hostile environment SH actions. State provisions offering protection on the basis of sexual orientation are discussed as are employer defenses to charges of homosexual harassment.

411. Norris, William P. "Liberal attitudes and homophobic acts: The paradoxes of homosexual experience in a liberal institution." *Journal of Homosexuality* 22:3/4 (1991), 81-120.

This article details research done at Oberlin College concerning the victimization of and attitudes toward lesbians, gay men, and bisexuals. Students as well as employees were surveyed and their experiences are reported. The author found a paradox of considerable victimization yet strong attitudinal support. Theoretical explanations for this paradox are offered. (10 refs).

412. Ontiveros, Maria L. "Three perspectives on workplace harassment of woman of color." *Golden Gate University Law Review* 23:3 (Summer 1993), 817-828.

Issues of race and culture as they pertain to SH cases are examined, as are the perspective of the harasser, the victim, and the judicial system. The author argues that race or national origin affect the way a victim is perceived by the harasser and can also affect the resolution of the case by the court.

413. White, Jean Ella. "Sexual harassment in the workplace." Dissertation, Kansas State University, 1990.

13

Sexual Harassment in Housing

414. Aalberts, Robert J. "Preventing sexual harassment in housing." *Journal of Property Management* 58:6 (November/December 1993), 52-55.

   Aalberts argues that a well-written SH policy and effective implementation of such policy might not only prevent SH from happening, but can also place the owner in a position to discover it if SH does occur and deal with it in a timely manner. A model policy for dealing with SH of tenants is proposed.

415. Aalberts, Robert J., and Terrence M. Clauretie. "Sexual harassment in housing." *Journal of Property Management* 57:1 (January/February 1992), 44-47.

   Following a review of the Fair Housing Act, the authors focus on the 1985 *Shellhammer v. Lewallen* case, the first to apply the Fair Housing Act to SH in housing.

416. Butler, Kathleen. "Sexual harassment in rental housing." *University of Illinois Law Review* 1989:1 (Winter 1989), 175-214.

   The women's housing crisis includes women vulnerable to SH by landlords. This problem, and the remedies under the Fair Housing Law, is the focus of this article. In addition, the author advocates educational programs and forms of relief that protect plaintiffs from retaliation.

417. Cahan, Regina. "Home is no haven: An analysis of sexual harassment in housing." *Wisconsin Law Review* 6 (November-December 1987), 1061-1093.

The nature and scope of SH in housing are examined in this article. Results of a 1986 survey of 87 fair housing agencies from across the country include 288 reported incidents of SH in housing from 57 centers but none from the other 30. Existing legal mechanisms for addressing SH in housing as well as new avenues for litigating this type of claim are also discussed.

418.   Rosenthal, Robert. "Landlord sexual harassment: A federal remedy." *Temple Law Review* 65:2 (Summer 1992), 589-613.

SH of tenants by their landlords is the focus of this article. The author looks at the definition and increase of landlord SH, and SH as a cause of action against landlords. Related details of Title VII and the Fair Housing Act are included.

14

Elements of a Sexual Harassment Claim under Title VII: Quid Pro Quo, Hostile Environment, and the Issues of Reasonableness and Welcomeness

419. Adams, Todd B. "Universalism and sexual harassment." *Oklahoma Law Review* 44:4 (December 22 1991), 683-694.

Adams is a proponent for a reasonable person standard, which clearly and specifically addresses the realities of SH for men and women, as the means to best advance justice. Criticism of the reasonable woman and reasonable victim standards is also presented.

420. Adler, Robert S., and Ellen R. Peirce. "The legal, ethical, and social implications of the "reasonable woman" standard in sexual harassment cases." *Fordham Law Review* 61:4 (March 1993), 773-827.

Legal, ethical, and social issues raised by the use of the reasonable woman standard are examined in this article. The authors discuss several potential problems related to this change in policy that should be considered by the courts, in particular the question of whether it is fair to hold men to a standard of conduct they many not understand.

421. Alvarado, Karen Ann Hansen. "Sexual harassment: Implementation of federal policy." Dissertation, University of Oregon, 1988.

422. Ashraf, Saba. "The reasonableness of the "reasonable woman" standard: An evaluation of its use in hostile environment sexual harassment claims under Title VII of the Civil Rights Act." *Hofstra Law Review* 21:2 (Winter 1992), 483-504.

After a historical introduction to the reasonable woman standard, the author discusses whether such a standard is needed, whether it is useful, and whether it should be continued. The author presents several reasons why the reasonable person standard should be retained.

423.   Barton, Christopher P. "Between the boss and a hard place: A consideration of *Meritor Savings Bank, FSB v. Vinson* and the law of sexual harassment." *Boston University Law Review* 67:3 (May 1987), 445-474.

   Meritor v. Vinson is used to illustrate the development of SH law and to suggest a direction for further change. The author reviews two issues not resolved by Vinson- employer liability and the treatment of unwelcomeness. The author goes on to argue for employer liability and the development of a jurisprudence of welcomeness that would significantly reduce unwanted sexual advances in the workplace.

424.   Bass, Stuart L. "The reasonable woman standard: The Ninth Circuit decrees sexes perceive differently." *Labor Law Journal* 43:7 (July 1992), 449-455.

   During recent hostile environment SH decisions, in particular *Ellison v. Brady*, courts have used the reasonable woman standard. The author asserts that courts should evaluate conduct from a reasonable victim perspective which would protect both men and women.

425.   Blackwood, Eileen M. "The reasonable woman in sexual harassment law and the case for subjectivity." *Vermont Law Review* 16:3 (Spring 1992), 1005-1026.

   Following a review of several court cases addressing the objective standards for SH liability, the author argues that courts must address the subjective nature of the harm involved in SH if they want to fully address the concerns of women.

426.   Brown, Barbara Berish, and Intra L. Germanis. "Hostile environment sexual harassment: Has Harris really changed things?" *Employee Relations Law Journal* 19:4 (Spring 1994), 567-578.

   The authors encourage employers to consider the Supreme Court's opinion in the 1993 *Harris v. Forklift* case, paying particular attention to the elimination of hostile environment situations and the provision of appropriate disciplinary procedures for violation of company SH policies.

427.   Bull, Christina A. "The implications of admitting evidence of a sexual harassment plaintiff's speech and dress in the aftermath of *Meritor Savings Bank v. Vinson.*" *UCLA Law Review* 41 (October 1993), 117-151.

   This article assesses the impact of the landmark *Meritor* case in which the court allowed evidence of the plaintiff's dress and speech to be admitted. Bull argues that admissibility of such irrelevant evidence discourages women from reporting SH, and leads to a review of the viticm's conduct rather than the defendant's.

428.   Carrillo, Maria M. "Hostile environment sexual harassment by a supervisor under Title VII: Reassessment of employment liability in light of the Civil Rights Act of 1991." *Columbia Human Rights Law Review* 24:1 (Winter 1992), 41-92.

Carrillo first examines Title VII causes for action against SH and the standard of employer liability it imposes. She then focuses on her theory that, by imposing vicarious liability, the courts would not only be supporting the goals of Title VII and the Civil Rights Act of 1991, but would also show their belief that SH is a serious social problem.

429.   Chan, Anja Angelica. *Women and Sexual Harassment: A Guide to the Legal Protections of Title VII and the Hostile Environment Claim.* New York: Hayworth Press, 1993.

This volume is meant to serve as a research tool for those investigating the hostile environment claim under Title VII. A legal history of hostile environment SH, the definition of it, remedies, statutes of limitations, and evidence are all covered in this pathfinder. The author includes a guide to cases, federal statutes and regulations, books and journal articles, and appropriate databases to search to retrieve additional information.

430.   Childers, Jolynn. "Is there a place for a reasonable woman in the law? A discussion of recent developments in hostile environment sexual harassment." *Duke Law Journal* 42:4 (February 1993), 854-904.

Following a historical overview of hostile environment SH cases and an exploration of power dynamics in harassment situations, the author advocates a more plaintiff-specific reasonable victim standard. Adopting the standard, it is argued, would remove the focus from sexual stereotypes while adapting to workplace management changes.

431.   Conte, Alba. "Class action: Remedy for the hostile environment." *Trial* 28:7 (July 1992), 18-20, 25.

Conte advocates use of the class action claim which will help rid the workplace of SH, allow victims a collective voice, allow for efficient use of time and money, and protect against the retaliatory conduct common in SH cases.

432.   DeCosse, Sarah A. "Simply unbelievable: Reasonable women and hostile environment sexual harassment." *Law and Inequality: A Journal of Theory and Practice* 10:2/3 (June 1992), 285-309.

The strengths and weaknesses of the reasonable woman standard are explored in this article. While the standard permits a broader range of actionable SH claims, courts must recognize that many factors impact the female SH victim's experience, including her race, class, and education.

433.   Dennison, Lynn. "An argument for the reasonable woman standard in hostile environment claims." *Ohio State law Journal* 54:2 (April 1993), 473-496.

After examining several hostile environment SH decisions, the author addresses criticisms of the reasonable woman standard and concludes that, although imperfect, it takes a step in the right direction.

434.   Dolkart, Jane L. "Hostile environment harassment: Equality, objectivity, and the shaping of legal standards." *Emory Law Journal* 43:1 (Winter 1994), 151-244.

Harris v. Forklift Systems, Inc. provides a backdrop as Dolkart discusses the shortcomings of the reasonableness standard and proposes an individualized standard for determining what conduct constitutes hostile environment sexual harassment. An individualized standard, she argues, would focus on the conduct of the harasser and not on the life and background of the victim.

435.   Ehrenreich, Nancy S. "Pluralist myths and powerless men: The ideology of reasonableness in sexual harassment law." *Yale Law Journal* 99:6 (April 1990), 1177-1234.

This article describes the role of reasonableness in recent hostile environment SH cases. By addressing individualist and pluralist approaches to SH, the author argues that our vision of pluralism needs to acknowledge the existence of conflict between groups, and the unavoidable nature of choices among them.

436.   Fechner, Holly B. "Toward an expanded conception of law reform: Sexual harassment law and the reconstruction of facts." *University of Michigan Journal of Law Reform* 23:3 (Spring 1990), 475-505.

The feminist methodology of consciousness raising is examined in this article. Based heavily on the writings of Catharine MacKinnon, feminist reform of SH law is used to illustrate how legal decision makers think about facts which can lead to law reform.

437. Fujiwara, Elizabeth Jubin. "Proving damages in a sexual harassment case." *Trial* 30:4 (April 1994), 34-37.

Several suggestions for lawyers who represent SH victims are offered. Recommended techniques for proving damages include: look at the events from a reasonable woman's perspective, recommend that the client see a mental health professional, obtain expert testimony, conduct thorough interviews, identify any prior emotional difficulties, and believe in the client.

438. Gehring, Thomas J. "Hostile work environment sexual harassment after Harris: Abolishing the requirement of psychological injury, *Harris v. Forklift Systems, Inc.*" *Thurgood Marshall Law Review* 19:2 (Spring 1994), 451-474.

This article focuses on the claim of hostile environment SH and what is needed to sustain a cause of action under Title VII. Gehring argues that the long overdue decision of the Harris court sends a clear message to employers: if you create a hostile working environment due to SH, you will suffer the consequences. Thanks to the Harris decision, SH victims will have a less stringent standard to meet when proving Title VII violations.

439. George, B. Glenn. "The back door: Legitimizing sexual harassment claims." *Boston University Law Review* 73:1 (January 1993), 1-38.

The author contends that courts have conveyed ambiguous messages about the seriousness and viability of SH claims by placing numerous legal obstacles in the plaintiff's path. The existence of obstacles such as pervasiveness, unwelcomeness, and sexual nature, contrasts dramatically with other types of Title VII claims.

440. Gomez, Mary C. "Sexual harassment after *Harris v. Forklift Systems, Inc.*- Is it really easier to prove?" *Nova Law Review* 18:3 (Spring 1994), 1891-1917.

Gomez provides an overview of Title VII before turning the focus of the article to the *Harris v. Forklift Systems, Inc.* decisions. Two conflicts resolved by the Harris case are discussed: the adoption of the modified reasonable person test and the removal of the psychological harm requirement. The removal of the latter ensures that plaintiffs need not endure a nervous breakdown as part of their proof of SH.

441. Greene, Sheryl A. "Reevaluation of Title VII abusive environment claims based on sexual harassment after *Meritor Savings Banks v. Vinson.*" *Thurgood Marshall Law Review* 13:1/2 (Fall/Spring 1988), 29-65.

Following a review of discrimination law under Title VII, the author proposes a modified agency law standard identical to standards imposed on discrimination cases other than SH. This modified standard would protect both the employers and the victims of SH. The author goes on to suggest that the courts must interpret Title VII to include damages for the psychological harm inflicted upon the victim of hostile environment SH.

442. Hipp, E. Clayton, Jr. "Now you see it, now you don't: The "hostile work environment" after *Meritor." American Business Law Journal* 26:2 (Summer 1988), 339-361.

The author utilizes several recent hostile environment decisions to illustrate the lack of a clear definition of a hostile environment and to demonstrate that, unless the Supreme Court clarifies its stance in this area, lower courts will continue to face uncertainty.

443. Johnson, Paul B. "The reasonable woman in sexual harassment law: Progress or illusion?" *Wake Forest Law Review* 28:3 (September 1993), 619-669.

Philosophical and practical problems of the reasonable woman standard are explored by the author. Johnson argues that the reasonable woman standard is unsound and should be discarded, and focus should be turned to the reasonableness of the defendants' conduct.

444. Juliano, Ann C. "Did she ask for it? The "unwelcome" requirement in sexual harassment cases." *Cornell Law Review* 77:6 (September 1992), 1558-1592.

The author explores the unwelcomeness issue and stresses that the definition and evidence of unwelcomeness must be carefully regulated. The author also contends that the court's requirements for unwelcome conduct invokes stereotypes and stagnates Title VII.

445. Kirk, Delaney J. "Hostile environment: A discriminant model of the perceptions of working women." Dissertation, University of North Texas, 1988.

446. Koen, Clifford M. "Sexual harassment: Criteria for defining hostile environment." *Employee Responsibilities and Rights Journal* 2:4 (December 1989), 289-301.

The author reviews several SH cases decided since the 1986 *Meritor v. Vinson* decision. The cases illustrate the wide variety of verbal and physical conduct that can constitute a claim of hostile environment and render an employer liable for SH.

447. Lester, Toni. "The reasonable woman test in sexual harassment law- Will it really make a difference?" *Indiana Law Review* 26:2 (Spring 1993), 227-262.

This article focuses on the characteristics of both the reasonable person and reasonable woman standards used in hostile environment claims. The author applies the reasonable woman test to five cases that had previously been rejected. An analysis of these cases reveals that all but one of the plaintiffs would have won had the reasonable woman test been used.

448. Levy, Anne C. "Sexual harassment cases in the 1990s: "Backlashing" the "backlash" through Title VII." *Albany Law Review* 56:1 (Fall 1992), 1-51.

The author presents a descriptive overview of SH in the early 1990s, explores the phenomenon of SH itself, and reviews the psychology of power struggles in the workplace.

449. Lindemann, Barbara Schlei, and David D. Kadue. *Sexual Harassment in Employment Law*. Washington, DC: Bureau of National Affairs, 1992.

This book provides a more thorough examination of SH law than the authors' *Primer on Sexual Harassment* (1992). Discussed are forms of SH, theories of liability, preventive and remedial action, and litigation strategies. The appendices include sample SH policies, a review of the Civil Rights Act of 1991, and the EEOC Guidelines on SH. A comprehensive table of cases is also presented.

450. Marcus, Eric H. "Sexual harassment claims: Who is a reasonable woman?" *Labor Law Journal* 44:10 (October 1993), 646-650.

The author contends that the reasonable woman standard provides no practical benefit over the purportedly male-biased reasonable person standard. He advocates a modification of the reasonable person standard that would take into account the individual's beliefs and ideals. He also explores the forensic interview as it is utilized to determine health-related damages.

451. Maschke, Karen J. *Litigation, Courts, and Women Workers*. New York, NY: Praeger Publishers, 1989.

Maschke uses case examples to illustrate how litigation has shaped the concept of sexual discrimination, particularly SH. Title VII, the EEOC Guidelines, and the litigation process are discussed.

452. Maschke, Karen J. *Litigation, Courts, and Women Workers.* New York: Praeger Publishers, 1989.

Maschke uses case examples to illustrate how litigation has shaped the concept of sexual discrimination, particularly SH. Title VII, the EEOC Guidelines, and the litigation process are discussed.

453. Mays, Shirley L. "Sexual harassment and the law: Justice or "just us"." *Capital University Law Review* 22 (Summer 1993), 623-639.

The author suggests that, with the approach of the twenty-first century, we must bring SH law in line with reality or risk supporting institutions that continue to hamper a woman's ability to work in an environment free of gender biases. Male dominance, gender perspective, and the dispensation of justice are examined.

454. McCaslin, Leah R. "*Harris v. Forklift Systems, Inc.*: Defining the plaintiff's burden in hostile environment sexual harassment claims." *Tulsa Law Journal* 29:3/4 (Spring/Summer 1994), 761-779.

This article chronicles the legal battle of Teresa Harris following the terminiation of her employment with Forklift Systems, Inc. After lower court rejection of her case, the Supreme Court found in favor of Harris. McCaslin supports the adoption by the Supreme Court of the modified reasonable person standard and the removal of the proof of psychological suffering requirement.

455. Medlin, Nell J. "Expanding the law of sexual harassment to include workplace pornography: *Robinson v. Jacksonville Shipyards, Inc.*" *Stetson Law Review* 21:2 (Spring 1992), 655-680.

The author explores those SH rulings which found that pornography contributes to a hostile environment. *Robinson v. Jacksonville Shipyards* is but one related decision discussed in this article.

456. Mogan, Cathleen Marie. "Current hostile environmental sexual harassment law: Time to stop defendants from having their cake and eating it too." *Notre Dame Journal of Law, Ethics & Public Policy* 6:2 (Summer 1992), 543-581.

Mogan addresses several questions left unanswered in hostile environment SH claims. Discussed are: tensions between the rights of SH victims and the harasser's right to free speech; between Title VII and state tort law; and between policies of equality and compensation. She advocates for the reform of Title VII and a separate tort for SH at the state level.

457. Morlacci, Maria. "Sexual harassment law and the impact of Vinson." *Employee Relations Law Journal* 13:3 (Winter 1987/1988), 501-519.

    Following a review of several influential SH court cases, the author discusses the psychological effects of SH in the workplace and the remedies available to victims under Title VII.

458. Nordin, Kathleen. "*Ellison v. Brady*: Is the reasonable woman test the solution to the problem of how best to evaluate hostile environment sexual harassment claims?" *Western State University Law Review* 19:2 (Spring 1992), 607-622.

    This article looks at the reasonable woman standard, utilized in *Ellison v. Brady*, from three perspectives of feminist legal theory: equality theory, difference theory, and postmodernism.

459. Paetzold, Ramona L., and Bill Shaw. "A postmodern feminist view of "reasonableness" in hostile environment sexual harassment." *Journal of Business Ethics* 13:9 (September 1994), 681-691.

    Two separate points of view regarding reasonableness and welcomeness are presented in this article. One author argues that reasonableness reinforces social norms of conformity, serves to devalue emotion, and preserves male privilege in law. The second author advocates that reasonableness, albeit not perfect, can work. The authors agree that the male-bias so pervasive in the workplace and the legal system must be eliminated.

460. Patterson, James M. "Sexual harassment in the workplace: The continuing quest for the reasonable woman standard." *American Journal of Trial Advocacy* 15:2 (Winter 1991), 415-433.

    Details the reasonable woman standard and the hostile environment claim. The author suggests that in hostile environment cases, the courts should examine the claim from the standpoint of a reasonable victim.

461. Pechman, Louis. "Emerging issues in hostile work environment sexual harassment." *New York State Bar Journal* 65 (March/April 1993), 38-41, 59.

    Pechman, an experienced labor and employment specialist, explores several areas of SH believed to warrant close examination. Discussed are: alternative perspectives for determining SH, prevalent commercial and societal norms, and gender differences. The impact of the Civil Rights Act of 1991 is also discussed.

462. Pinkston, David L. "Redefining objectivity: The case for the reasonable woman standard in hostile environment claims." *Brigham Young University Law Review* 1993:1 (Winter 1993), 363-383.

The author uses the *Ellision v. Brady* decision to illustrate that women see sexual conduct differently than men. Pinkston suggests that adoption of the reasonable woman standard is the most effective way to gain an understanding of what conduct offends SH victims.

463. Radford, Mary F. "By invitation only: The proof of welcomeness in sexual harassment cases." *North Carolina Law Review* 72:3 (March 1994), 499-548.

Professor Radford proposes an alternative element by which welcomeness rather than unwelcomeness must be proved in cases of SH. More specifically, she argues that the burden of proving welcomeness should be shifted from the complainant to the aggressor.

464. Reilly, Marie T. "A paradigm for sexual harassment: Toward the optimal level of loss." *Vanderbilt Law Review* 47:2 (March 1994), 427-476.

The author examines the costs of SH precaution vs. the expected loss. Based on the negligence rule known as the Hand Formula, Reilly advocates a paradigm which encourages women to achieve the optimal level of precaution against loss. The paradigm is applied to both quid pro quo and hostile environment SH.

465. Rizzolo, Nicole D. "A right with questionable bite: The future of "abusive or hostile work environment" sexual harassment as a cause of action for women in a gender-biased society and legal system." *New England Law Review* 23:1 (Summer 1988), 263-290.

Rizzolo points to recent improvements in the treatment of women in the legal system and offers her own remedial suggestions. Adoption of a clear definition of SH and the creation of a task force to study gender bias in the courtroom are two of her recommendations.

466. "Sexual harassment claims of abusive work environment under Title VII." *Harvard Law Review* 97:6 (April 1984), 1449-1467.

Presents a legal representation of hostile environment that urges the courts to identify the hostile or abusive environment claims as either facial sex discrimination or disparate impact. It could be treated as facially discriminatory as SH is based on the employee's sex; the disparate impact approach would need only the establishment of the existence of an abusive environment.

467.   Shaney, Mary Jo. "Perceptions of harm: The consent defense in sexual harassment cases." *Iowa Law Review* 71 (May 1986), 1109-1135.

The issue of consent in SH cases is examined in this article. Several relevant court cases are used to illustrate the consent standards that have been utilized. The author suggests an overt consent standard which would require courts to focus on whether the victim consented to sexual conduct rather than on whether the victim resisted the harasser's behavior.

468.   Sperry, Martha. "Hostile environment sexual harassment and the imposition of liability without notice: A progressive approach to traditional gender roles and power based relationships." *New England Law Review* 24:3 (Spring 1990), 917-952.

In the case of *College-Town, Division of Interco, Inc. v. Massachusetts Commission Against Discrimination*, the court's position was that an employer can be held liable for the discriminatory acts of agents and supervisors. The author uses this case to illustrate and focus on the issues of hostile environment SH and employer liability.

469.   Stark, Sheldon J. "Sexual harassment in the workplace: Lessons from the Thomas-Hill hearings." *Trial* 28:5 (May 1992), 116-122.

Stark traces the struggling evolution of SH case law, with particular emphasis on the legal climate of 1981 when Anita Hill allegedly experienced SH. The author describes the personal, professional, and political obstacles Hill would have faced had she brought charges of SH against Thomas, one of the highest black officials in the federal government. Stark argues that the law of SH has a great deal of maturing to do.

470.   Staton, Georgia A., and Angela K. Sinner "Sexual harassment: The "reasonable woman" standard." *For the Defense* (December 1991), 6-10.

The authors describe the evolution of the reasonable woman standard, with particular emphasis on the 1991 *Ellison v. Brady* decision. The authors support the *Ellison* court's standard which is based on the perception of a reasonable person of the same sex as the alleged victim. The authors hope this standard will eventually lead to a less hostile workplace.

471.   Sutton, Geraldine Spears. "Sexual harassment of women in the workplace and in academe: Legal redress." Dissertation, Pepperdine University, 1987.

472. Thomann, Daniel A. "The utility of a legal model of attributions of responsibility for sexual harassment grievances." Dissertation, Saint Louis Universtiy, 1985.

473. Torres, David A. "Judicial interpretation of sexual harassment regulations." Dissertation, University of Nevada, Reno, 1992.

474. Treger, Tracy L. "The reasonable woman? Unreasonable!!! *Ellison v. Brady.*" *Whittier Law Review* 14:3 (September 1993), 675-694.

After a brief review of the background of hostile environment SH, including the *Ellison v. Brady* decision, the author focuses on the problems associated with using the reasonable woman standard to analyze hostile environment cases.

475. Vinciguerra, Marlisa. "The aftermath of *Meritor*: A search for standards in the law of sexual harassment." *Yale Law Journal* 98:8 (June 1989), 1717-1738.

Meritor v. Vinson acts as a backdrop for analyzing the framework courts apply to quid pro quo and hostile environment SH. Vinciguerra proposes a methodology for recognizing the subtle differences between the two causes of action.

476. Wells, Deborah L., and Beverly J. Kracher. "Justice, sexual harassment, and the reasonable victim standard." *Journal of Business Ethics: JBE* 12:6 (June 1993), 423-431.

Wells and Kracher use the modern moral theory of John Rawls to support their argument that morality is a relevant source of standards for cases of hostile environment SH. Moral reasons for adopting the reasonable victim perspective are explored. (18 refs).

477. Westman, Bonnie B. "The reasonable woman standard: Preventing sexual harassment in the workplace." *William Mitchell Law Review* 18:3 (Summer 1992), 795-828.

This article first presents a historical overview of SH as a cause of action. The author then turns to the reasonable woman standard as a means of reducing SH and creating greater equality in the workplace.

15

A Legal Dilemma: Sexual Harassment and the First Amendment Rights to Privacy and Free Speech

478. Baer, Lawrence J., Stacey L. Davidson, and Deborah S. K. Jagoda. "Discovering sexual relations- Balancing the fundamental right to privacy against the need for discovery in a sexual harassment case." *New England Law Review* 25:3 (Spring 1991), 849-857.

This article explores the need to balance the seemingly incompatible interests of preserving an individual's rights to privacy pertaining to sexual conduct with the interests of full disclosure and discovery needs of the plaintiff in a SH case. *Boler v. Solano County Superior Court,* a case which addresses this matter, is discussed.

479. Browne, Kingsley. "Title VII as censorship: Hostile-environment harassment and the First Amendment." *Ohio State Law Journal* 52:2 (1991), 481-550.

Browne contends that the broad, vague definition of SH adopted by the courts has established a restriction of expression inconsistent with rights to free speech. He argues for the elimination of the ability to base hostile environment SH claims on expression.

480. Collins, Michael E. "Pin-ups in the workplace- balancing Title VII mandates with the right of free speech." *Cumberland Law Review* 23:3 (Spring 1993), 629-654.

This article focuses on the hostile work environment, specifically the posting of pictures that contain nudity. A review of judicial approaches to nudity in the workplace and recommendations for the free speech standard are included.

481.   Horton, Amy. "Of supervision, centerfolds, and censorship: Sexual harassment, the First Amendment, and the contours of Title VII." *University of Miami Law Review* 46:2 (November 1991), 403-453.

Following a review of *Robinson v. Jacksonville Shipyards, Inc.*, this article focuses on the First Amendment as a defense against SH claims. Issues such as free speech, employer control, and pinups in the workplace are explored.

482.   Klein, Susan R. "A survey of evidence and discovery rules in civil sexual harassment suits with special emphasis on California law." *Industrial Relations Law Journal* 11:4 (Winter 1990), 540-577.

This article examines state and federal rules of discovery and evidence pertaining to SH cases. The author suggests that the defendant's use of discovery and evidence in open court is unnecessary and may even be detrimental to the well being of the alleged SH victim. The author also advocates additional reform in the use of court ordered psychiatric exams.

483.   Laddy, Donna L. *"Burns v. McGregor Electronic Industries*: A per se rule against admitting evidence of general sexual expression as a defense to sexual harassment claims." *Iowa Law Review* 78:4 (May 1993), 939-964.

Laddy advocates that courts not allow discovery and presentation of evidence concerning the SH victim's dress and conduct outside of the workplace when the behavior does not involve co-workers. The *Burns v. McGregor Electronic Industries* case is reviewed under recent statutes covering the admissibility of such evidence in SH cases.

484.   "Pornography, equality, and a discrimination-free workplace: A comparative perspective." *Harvard Law Review* 106:5 (January 1993), 1075-1092.

This article explores how pornography in the workplace creates a hostile environment, therefore violating Title VII. The direct effects of pornography on women and a review of cases such as *Robinson v. Jacksonville Shipyards, Inc.*, are included.

16

Beyond Federal Remedies: State Common Law Torts and Other Sources of Recovery

485. Claypoole, Theodore F. "Inadequacies in civil rights law: The need for sexual harassment legislation." *Ohio State Law Journal* 48:4 (Fall 1987), 1151-1170.

   Claypoole argues that Congress should pass federal legislation to prohibit SH. Three reasons for the need of such legislation are: 1) SH has rapidly become an important social and legal issue; 2) courts and agencies are not equipped to handle the issue; and 3) Congress has yet to specifically address it.

486. Conte, Alba. *Sexual Harassment in the Workplace: Law and Practice, 2d ed., 2 vols.* New York: John Wiley and Sons, Inc., 1994.

   In volume 1 of this 2 volume publication, Conte documents such issues as: current elements of SH claims, employer defenses, available remedies, and implications of the Civil Rights Act of 1991. The second volume examines aspects of SH law in the 50 states and the District of Columbia. State antidiscrimination statutes, common law claims, and relevant case law are presented. Sample SH policies are among the items found in the appendices.

487. Conte, Alba. "State remedies for sexual harassment at work: Reconciling tort and workers' compensation laws." *Trial* 29:11 (November 1993), 56-61.

   Common law tort claims that are available at the state level include: assault, intentional infliction of emotional distress, and invasion of privacy. The author suggests that victims learn of their various options before filing a SH claim.

488. Douglas, Frederick L. "The Civil Rights Act of 1991: Continuing violation and the retroactivity controversy." *Labor Law Journal* 44:3 (March 1993), 153-161.

This article explores the general requirements to sustain a SH claim, and discusses the lack of consistency by the courts as to whether the 1991 Act should apply to pre-Act conduct.

489. Dworkin, Terry M., Laura Ginger, and Jane P. Mallor. "Theories of recovery for sexual harassment: Going beyond Title VII." *San Diego Law Review* 25:1 (January 1988), 125-159.

The advantages and disadvantages of employing theories of recovery for SH outside Title VII are presented. Theories such as traditional tort actions and actions under the Racketeer Influenced and Corrupt Organizations Act (RICO) are examined.

490. Faccenda, Susan M. "The emerging law of sexual harassment: Relief available to the public employee." *Notre Dame Law Review* 62:4 (1987), 677-687.

The avenues of relief available to public employees who are SH victims are discussed. Because of limitations in Title VII and state tort law, the author advocates for a clear state policy prohibiting SH in the workplace.

491. Goodson, Jane, Christine Lewis, and Renee Culverhouse. "The tort of outrage: How sexual harassment victims are fight back." *Human Rights* 20:2 (Spring 1993), 10-13, 30.

This article uses case examples to show that SH victims may win more damage awards by using worker's compensation or the intentional infliction tort. Also discussed are mental injuries arising from SH and often recognized by the Courts.

492. Korn, Jane Byeff. "The fungible woman and other myths of sexual harassment." *Tulane Law Review* 67:5 (May 1993), 1363-1419.

The author examines policy issues underlying the determination by many courts that workers' compensation is the exclusive remedy for SH. After a review of Title VII, tort remedies, and workers' compensation, Korn concludes that workers' compensation statutes were never intended to cover injuries from SH. SH, she argues, is not comparable to malfunctioning equipment or wet floors.

493. Lewis, Darryll M. Halcomb. "Sexual harassment under worker's compensation law." *Labor Law Journal* 44:5 (May 1993), 297-306.

The applicability of worker's compensation to SH claims is discussed in this article. After a review of various judicial approaches to this issue, the author proposes that states exclude worker's compensation claims based on SH.

494. Mathews, Susan M. "Title VII and sexual harassment: Beyond damages control." *Yale Journal of Law and Feminism* 3:2 (Spring 1991), 299-320.

Mathews asserts that, while the 1991 Civil Rights Act is likely to provide more adequate compensation to SH victims, they will continue to face additional problems in the courts concerning evidence and standards of proof.

495. Paul, Ellen Frankel. "Sexual harassment as sex discrimination: A defective paradigm." *Yale Law & Policy Review* 8:2 (Fall 1990), 333-365.

After a review of Title VII, the EEOC guidelines, and a number of SH cases, the author details a new tort approach to SH focusing on the individual rights of the victim and the individual liability of the harasser.

496. Schneider, Beth E. "Approaches, assaults, attractions, affairs: Policy implications of the sexualization of the workplace." *Population Research and Policy Review* 4:2 (June 1985), 93-113.

Schneider conceptualizes the sexualization of the workplace as sexual interactions at work which are either consensual or coerced. Since SH typically occurs to women and has a negative impact on women's emotional and psychological health as well as their financial condition, she argues that current legal remedies for SH are limited in their impact in effecting the changes needed to create fully equal female employees and self-directed women. She further suggests considering SH a workplace safety issue. (70 refs).

497. Schoenheider, Krista J. "A theory of tort liability for sexual harassment in the workplace." *University of Pennsylvania Law Review* 134:6 (July 1986), 1461-1495.

Schoenhelder advocates the development of an alternative tort claim for SH that would result in more equitable recovery for plaintiffs and a powerful deterrent to harassment in the workplace.

498. Spangler, Eve. "Sexual harassment: Labor relations by other means." *New Solutions: A Journal of Environmental and Occupational Health Policy* 3:1 (1992), 23-30.

The author has identified SH as a costly workplace hazard that needs to be recognized by occupational health and safety specialists. She proposes a feminist framing for handling workplace sexual harassment. (44 refs).

499. Stauffer, Lucia C. "Sexual harassment in the workplace: Developments in state tort law." *Annual Survey of American Law* 1988:3 (September 1988), 779-824.

SH plaintiffs often seek damages under tort law because a wide range of punitive remedies are provided. This article describes several cases where employers have sought to bar tort claims by arguing that SH is a workplace injury, therefore workers' compensation provides the victims exclusive remedy.

500. Vhay, Michael D. "The harms of asking: Towards a comprehensive treatment of sexual harassment." *University of Chicago Law Review* 55:1 (Winter 1988), 328-362.

After a review of the difficulties encountered in SH court cases, including the discomfort of dealing with matters of a sexual nature, the author contends that SH reflects both personal and societal difficulties. Tort remedies, education, and greater relief for victims are also stressed.

501. Wolman, Benson A. "Verbal sexual harassment on the job as intentional infliction of emotional distress." *Capital University Law Review* 17:2 (Fall 1988), 245-272.

This article focuses on the expansion of tort law to include causes of action for intentional and persistent use of outrageous and sexually-hostile language in the workplace. A definition, history, and overview of the tort of intentional infliction of emotional distress is presented.

17
___

Workplace Strategies: Arbitration and Negotiation

502. Baker, Chris. "Sexual harassment v. labor arbitration: Does reinstating sexual harassers violate public policy?" *University of Cincinnati Law Review* 61:4 (Spring 1993), 1361-1389.

The issue of whether courts should enforce arbitral awards that reinstate sexual harassers is the focus of this article. The author contends that although these procedures can slow down elimination of SH, they are still an effective way to handle the problem.

503. Costello, Edward J., Jr. "The mediation alternative in sex harassment cases." *Arbitration Journal* 47:1 (March 1992), 16-23.

The author, himself a mediator, contends that mediation is a quicker, more confidential, less expensive method of SH dispute resolution than court litigation. Examples of successful mediation cases are provided.

504. Crow, Stephen M., and Clifford M. Koen. "Sexual harassment: New challenge for labor arbitrators?" *Arbitration Journal* 47:2 (June 1992), 6-18.

The authors use Daugherty's seven tests of just cause and elaborate on the tests as a conceptual framework to develop both the legal and arbitration standards for determining SH. Daugherty's test includes: forewarning of possible disciplinary consequences of SH conduct, reasonable organizational rules, proper investigation of SH situations, evidence to support the accusation, equal treatment, and reasonable treatment.

505.   Gadlin, Howard. "Careful maneuvers: Mediating sexual harassment."
       Negotiation Journal 7:2 (April 1991), 139-153.

       The author relates his experience mediating SH grievances as the
       ombudsperson at the University of Massachusetts, Amhurst. The
       reasons why mediation is appropriate for SH grievance procedures are
       given. The author offers two recommendations: individual sessions
       prior to joint sessions and encouraging the participants to use a
       support person throughout the process. (3 refs).

506.   Gwartney-Gibbs, Patricia A., and Denise H. Lach. "Sociological
       explanations for failure to seek sexual harassment remedies."
       Mediation Quarterly: Journal of the Academy of Family Mediators 9:4
       (Summer 1992), 365-374.

       Public and private debate over the Thomas-Hill hearings has centered
       on the psychology of the situation and Hill's state of mind in
       particular. No psychological examination, the authors contend, takes
       into account the influences of gender and race in the social organization
       of work. The concepts of tokenism, gender roles, and dispute
       resolution are used to explain why a woman, and in particular a
       minority woman, would wait ten years to pursue a claim of SH.

507.   Hauck, Vern E., and Thomas G. Pearce. "Sexual harassment and
       arbitration." *Labor Law Journal* 43:1 (January 1992), 31-39.

       Following a review of *Meritor Savings Bank v. Vinson*, the authors
       report the results of an in-depth analysis of 100 published SH
       arbitration awards. Findings indicated that complaints of a hostile
       working environment or unwelcome sexual advances occurred in 92%
       of the awards, and that guilty co-workers were discharged in only 15%
       of the cases.

508.   Holzman, Amy. "Denial of attorney's fees for claims of sexual harassment
       resolved through informal dispute resolution: A shield for employers, a
       sword against women." *Fordham Law Review* 63:1 (October 1994),
       245-279.

       Although informal dispute resolution offers SH victims the
       opportunity to resolve their claims in the most private manner, lower
       courts have recently denied recovery of attorney's fees for such
       resolutions. Holzman proposes amending Title VII to enable
       complainants to recover fees if their informal proceedings are
       successful.

509. Irvine, Mori. "Mediation: Is it appropriate for sexual harassment grievances?" *Ohio State Journal on Dispute Resolution* 9:1 (1993), 27-53.

"No" is Professor Irvine's answer to the question posed in the title of this article. While mediation can prove appropriate for some disputes, Irvine demonstrates that it is not a useful means of resolving SH disputes. Mediation, the author argues, risks trivializing the seriousness of SH, may result in reinstatement or a reduction in penalty for harassers, and may leave doubts in the workforce as to what conduct is permitted.

510. Meredith, Susan R. "Using fact finders to probe workplace claims of sexual harassment." *Arbitration Journal* 47:4 (December 1992), 61-65.

Following a review of common remedies for SH claims, such as arbitration and court litigation, Meredith explores an alternative effort offered by the American Arbitration and Award Association. This program provides male/female fact finding teams of experienced SH arbitrators to meet with all parties and make recommendations in a confidential manner.

511. Monat, Johathan S., and Angel Gomez. "Decisional standards used by arbitrators in sexual harassment cases." *Labor Law Journal* 37:10 (October 1986), 712-718.

In an examination of several SH arbitration cases, the authors illustrate the issues routinely faced by arbitrators: credibility, degree of SH, and employer liability. It is the authors' contention that arbitrators are well suited to handle such claims.

512. Nowlin, William A. "Sexual harassment in the workplace: How arbitrators rule." *Arbitration Journal* 43:4 (December 1988), 31-40.

This article focuses on several SH arbitration cases brought by both victims and alleged offenders. The cases reviewed show how care has been exercised in administering discipline to workers charged with SH. Based on his analysis of these cases, the author concludes with recommendations for labor and management to address this issue.

513. Oswald, Sharon L., and Steven B. Caudill. "Experimental evidence of gender effects in arbitration decisions." *Employee Responsibilities and Rights Journal* 4:4 (December 1991), 271-281.

In a study of 146 arbitrators (117 males and 29 females) who were asked to rule on a hypothetical SH case- half with female grievants, half with male grievants- results showed no significant evidence of gender effect on decisions. However, results did indicate that older, more experienced arbitrators are harsher on grievants than younger arbitrators. (24 refs).

514. Piskorski, Thomas J. "Reinstatement of the sexual harasser: The conflict between federal labor law and Title VII." *Employee Relations Law Journal* 18:4 (Spring 1993), 617-623.

Arguing that employers are in a dangerous dilemma because of two public policies- the public policy against SH and the policy favoring the private resolution of workplace disagreements- the author describes several court decisions and examines their rationale.

515. Rule, William S. "Arbitral standards in sexual harassment cases." *Industrial Relations Law Journal* 10:1 (Winter 1988), 12-18.

The author presents several examples of difficult questions and situations faced by arbitrators who deal with SH complaints. Two problems discussed are the determination of credibility and the interpretation of external law.

516. Sarles, Jeffrey. "The case of the missing woman: Sexual harassment and judicial review of arbitration awards." *Harvard Women's Law Journal* 17:1 (Spring 1994), 17-56.

Four recent circuit court cases reviewed arbitral reinstatements of sexual harassers. The author analyzes these cases and a concern for the need of increased judicial scrutiny of arbitral decisions which lack serious application by the arbitrator of the Title VII policy against SH. Sarles challenges the courts to review these cases in such a way as to protect the interests of victims and rights of discharged employees.

517. Stamato, Linda. "Sexual harassment in the workplace: Is mediation an appropriate forum?" *Mediation Quarterly: Journal of the Academy of Family Mediators* 10:2 (Winter 1992), 167-172.

Given that many victims of SH are refusing to report such incidents to avoid litigation and humiliating exposure, mediation may prove to be a desirable avenue of redress. Several reasons for considering mediation are given: mediation allows for respectful communication, it offers more immediate relief from harassment, and it is less costly than litigation. Consequently, Stamato argues, the use of mediation could also encourage the reporting of SH.

518. Williams, Andrea. "Model procedures for sexual harassment claims." *The Arbitration Journal* 48:3 (September 1993), 66-75.

Arguing that the current litigation process fails to meet the conflicting needs of all parties in a SH dispute, the author outlines what she believes to be a more efficient process for resolving SH claims. The benefits of the American Arbitration Association's model Sexual Harassment Claims Resolution Process is given, including: faster resolution, use of a male-female fact-finding team, and creative methods for addressing the emotional aspects of the case.

18

Process, Predictors, and Outcomes of Sexual Harassment Claims

519.   Binder, Renee L. "Sexual harassment: Issues for forensic psychiatrists."
       Bulletin of the American Academy of Psychiatry and the Law 20:4
       (December 1992), 409-418.

       Based on her experiences as an expert witness in 28 SH cases, the
       author examines the psychological and legal issues about which
       forensic psychiatrists may be consulted. These issues include whether
       the harassment occurred, the psychological effects of the harassment,
       the prognosis, and the treatment possibilities. Examples are used to
       illustrate how expert testimony can help determine damages related to
       the psychological effects of the sexual harassment.

520.   Bingham, Shereen G., and Lisa L. Scherer. "Factors associated with
       responses to sexual harassment and satisfaction with outcome." *Sex
       Roles* 29:3/4 (August 1993), 239-269.

       The authors describe results of a survey of 105 university faculty and
       staff members which examined the causal factors and responses to SH,
       as well as satisfaction with the outcome of the situation. Results
       indicated that employees responded more strongly to the behavior when
       it was perceived as SH and if the work environment was perceived as
       being conducive to SH. Talking with the harasser was associated with
       a satisfactory outcome; talking with friends or family was associated
       with a non-satisfactory outcome. (59 refs).

521.   Coles, Frances S. "Forced to quit: Sexual harassment complaints and
       agency response." *Sex Roles* 14:1/2 (January 1986), 81-95.

       This study reviews SH cases filed during a five-year period in
       California and the agency response or case outcomes. Thirty-six

percent of the complainants were over 30 years of age, dispelling the myth that SH is something that happens only to young women. However, the perpetrators were generally in positions of power, either owners or supervisors, and were often surprised that their behavior was illegal. Out of 88 cases, 42 were settled by the agency in less than three months, 21 cases were denied, and 18 complainants elected court action. A sample SH policy is appended. (24 refs).

522.   Coles, Frances S. "Sexual harassment: Complainant definitions and agency responses." *Labor Law Journal* 36:6 (June 1985), 369-376.

A study was performed of 88 SH complaints filed during a five-year period in San Bernardino County. In an examination of the perpetrators, complainants, and agency action, the author found that most complainants were under 35 years of age, most perpetrators were supervisors, and approximately one-half of all complaints were settled by the agency in less than 3 months.

523.   Egbert, J. Michael, Charles H. Moore, Karl L. Wuensch, and Wilbur A. Castellow. "The effect of litigant social desirability on judgments regarding a sexual harassment case." *Journal of Social Behavior and Personality* 7:4 (December 1992), 569-579.

One hundred sixty undergraduates read case information, then indicated their verdict and degree of defendant guilt. Cases were manipulated by varying the degree of social desirability of both victim and plaintiff. High social desirability was found to positively influence both the plaintiff's and the defendant's verdicts. Monetary awards, in cases of guilt, were affected to a significant degree by the plaintiff's social desirability.

524.   Feldman-Schorrig, Sara P., and James J. McDonald, Jr. "The role of forensic psychiatry in the defense of sexual harassment cases." *Journal of Psychiatry and Law* 20:1 (Spring 1992), 5-33.

The authors describe the use of a thorough forensic evaluation as a tool in defending a SH suit. Information regarding the plaintiff's background and mental status can be useful to determine if the plaintiff has exaggerated the situation, is hypersensitive to sexual cues, suffers from a personality disorder, or was psychologically injured as a result of SH. Case examples are included.

525.   Greenlaw, Paul S., and John P. Kohl. "Proving Title VII sexual harassment: The courts' view." *Labor Law Journal* 43:3 (March 1992), 164-171.

In order to prove SH under Title VII, the plaintiff has to meet five criteria: membership in a protected group, unwelcomeness, the harassment was based on sex, it was either quid pro quo and hostile environment SH, and employer liability. Because of the complications involved in proving hostile environment SH, the authors encourage legal scholars to pay particular attention to this type of SH.

526.   Hadsell, Barbara Enloe. "Keys to a successful plaintiff's settlement of a sexual harassment case." *National Lawyers Guild Practitioner* 49:2 (Spring 1992), 55-64.

According to the author, the most important element in a successful plaintiff's settlement of a SH case is an in-depth appreciation by counsel of the anguish a SH victim feels. Recommended is consultation with a psychologist or other medical expert, and consultation with an employment practices expert.

527.   Hadsell, Barbara Enloe. "Maximizing damages recovery in a sexual harassment case." *ALI-ABA Course Materials Journal* 17:2 (October 1992), 7-28.

The author stresses the importance of the plaintiff's attorney to be as knowledgeable as possible about the effects of SH on the client. She recommends that the plaintiff's attorney consult with SH experts, educate the client, educate the defendants, and assist the judge and jury in appreciating the seriousness of the situation.

528.   LaVan, Helen. "Decisional model for predicting outcomes of arbitrated sexual harassment disputes." *Labor Law Journal* 44:4 (April 1993), 230-238.

A study was performed in order to understand how SH is resolved in arbitration. A model was developed to be used as a predictor of the outcomes of SH arbitration. The author presents frequent case outcomes and characteristics related to the discharge of harassers.

529.   Lees-Haley, Paul R., and Stephanie Anderson. "The trauma of sexual harassment." *Trial Diplomacy Journal* 16:4 (July 1993), 151-155.

After reviewing the odds for a favorable SH case outcome and the circumstances surrounding the decision to file a complaint, the authors explore plaintiff credibility and the elements to consider when presenting the trauma of SH to a jury.

530.   Terpstra, David E. "The process and outcomes of sexual harassment
       claims." *Labor Law Journal* 44:10 (October 1993), 632-638.
       This article describes the process of filing formal SH charges and
       represents case variables that often influence the outcomes of court
       decisions. The information offered should be of use to both future
       complainants and organizations wishing to prevent lawsuits.

531.   Terpstra, David E., and Douglas D. Baker. "Outcomes of sexual
       harassment charges." *Academy of Management Journal* 31:1 (March
       1988), 185-194.

       The authors focus on nine key aspects which affect the settlement or
       dismissal of SH charges. Eighty-one SH cases filed under Title VII
       with the Illinois Department of Human Rights from July 1981
       through June 1983 were examined. The aspects explored include: the
       degree of sexual harassment, the relationship between harasser and
       harassee, notification of management of sexual harassment, and action
       taken by management when notified. Findings indicate that the
       plaintiff was more likely to receive a favorable outcome if the SH was
       severe, if management was notified prior to charges being filed, and if
       there were witnesses. (12 refs).

532.   Terpstra, David E., and Douglas D. Baker. "Outcomes of federal court
       decisions on sexual harassment." *Academy of Management Journal*
       35:1 (March 1992), 181-190.

       The authors examined the influences of 9 aspects on the outcomes of
       133 federal court cases of SH filed between 1974 and 1989. A
       comparison between these results and those of a previous study
       involving charges filed with the EEOC was made. Results of both
       studies were similar, and indicated that both documentation of SH and
       witnesses to the SH heavily influence case outcomes. (12 refs).

533.   Terpstra, David E., and Susan E. Cook. "Complainant characteristics and
       reported behaviors and consequences associated with formal sexual
       harassment charges." *Personnel Psychology* 38:3 (Fall 1985), 559-
       574.

       SH charges filed by 76 women and 5 men Illinois from 1981-1983
       were examined to determine the characteristics of the individuals who
       filed formal complaints and the employment-related consequences
       associated with these charges. Forty-three percent of the women were
       single. Those with a college degree or were employed in either a
       paraprofessional or technical area were over represented in this study.
       Sixty-five percent of the subjects reported job discharge. (28 refs).

534. York, Kenneth M. "A policy capturing analysis of federal district and appellate court sexual harassment cases." *Employee Responsibilities and Rights Journal* 5:2 (1992), 173-184.

The author describes a policy capturing study of 206 federal district and appellate cases to determine which factors judges use to define SH and how closely the information used matches EEOC Guidelines. The findings presented could be used by potential plaintiffs or defendants in SH cases to predict the likely outcome of their cases. (50 refs).

Appendix I: Sexual Harassment Chronology

1964 Title VII of the Civil Rights Act of 1964
      Title VII made it unlawful for an employer to discriminate based on an
      individuals' race, color, religion, sex, or national origin.

1972 Title IX of the Education Amendments of 1972
      Title IX provides that no person shall, on the basis of sex, be excluded
      from participation or be subjected to discrimination under any education
      program or activity receiving Federal financial assistance.

1974 Housing and Community Act Amendments of 1974
      Amendments to the Fair Housing Act of 1968, made it unlawful to
      discriminate, in the terms or conditions of the sale or lease of a home,
      based on sex.

1975 *Corne v. Bausch & Lomb*
      First introduced the issue of unwanted sexual advances to the courts.

1975 "Sexual Harassment"
      The phrase first became part of the English language.

1976 *Williams v. Saxbe*
      The first successful federal case in which sexual harassment was
      the chief complaint.

1976 Redbook Magazine National Survey on Sexual Harassment
      One of the earliest sexual harassment surveys. Reported that of 9,000
      women, 90% reported personal incidents of sexual harassment.

1979   MacKinnon, Catharine A. *Sexual Harassment of Working Women: A Case of Sex Discrimination.* New Haven: Yale University Press, 1979. MacKinnon's landmark publication on sexual harassment was credited with popularizing the term, increasing awareness of the problem, and influencing changes in the law.

1980   The Equal Employment Opportunity Commission's Guidelines on Sexual Discrimination
Declared sexual harassment a violation of Title VII, established criteria for determining when unwelcome conduct of a sexual nature constitutes sexual harassment, clarified the circumstances under which an employer may be held liable, and suggested steps employers should take to prevent sexual harassment.

1982   *Henson v. City of Dundee*
First case to propose strict employer liability for quid pro quo harassment, while requiring proof that the employer knew or should have known of harassment to apply strict liability in hostile environment cases.

1986   *Meritor Savings Bank, FSB v. Vinson*
In this, the Supreme Court's first treatment of sexual harassment, the court unanimously affirmed that sexual harassment is prohibited by Title VII. Also addressed the issue of unwelcome conduct.

1986   *Rabidue v. Osceola Refining Company*
Introduced the reasonable person standard into the evaluation of hostile environment claims. Additionally, the court held that to establish employer liability in a hostile environment claim, the plaintiff must show that the employer knew or should have known of the harassment and failed to take action.

1991   *Ellison v. Brady*
This court adopted the reasonable woman, or reasonable victim, standard of evaluation. The court also held that taking remedial actions to prevent sexual harassment can shield employers from liability.

1991   *Robinson v. Jacksonville Shipyards, Inc.*
Using the reasonable woman standard, the court held that the presence of sexually oriented pictures, or "pin ups", in the workplace combined with pervasive sexual comments by male coworkers constitutes sexual harassment.

1991   Thomas-Hill Hearings
Law Professor Anita Hill's now-famous allegations of sexual harassment against Supreme Court Nominee, Clarence Thomas. Hill's testimony

brought the issue of sexual harassment out in the open and into our living rooms.

1991 Civil Rights Act of 1991

This act, effective November 1991, provides that a plaintiff may recover awards for punitive and compensatory damages if it is demonstrated that the employer engaged in discriminatory practice with malice. Also entitles the plaintiff to trial by jury when seeking punitive or compensatory damages.

1993 *Harris v. Forklift Systems, Inc.*

The Supreme Court held unanimously that psychological injury does not have to be proven as an element of sexual harassment. Employees need only show a workplace permeated with discriminatory conduct sufficiently severe or pervasive enough to alter employment conditions.

Author Index

Subject Index

213, 215, 233; housing, 416; law
schools, 375; universities and
colleges, 10, 293, 305, 320, 324,
344, 372, 383, 387, 394, 397, 405;
workplace, 10, 23, 116, 128, 137,
143, 224, 243, 247, 252, 255, 268,
271, 273, 275, 278, 477, 497
Price Waterhouse v. Hopkins, 245
Prisoners of war, 87
Prisons, 153
Privacy, Right to, 241, 384, 478,
487
Productivity, 100, 185
Provocativenss, 50
Psychiatric evaluation, 450, 482,
519, 524
Psychiatric hospitals: staff, 196, 202
Psychiatric injury, 88
Psychological abuse, 187, 209, 491,
501
Psychological effects of SH. *See*
Emotional distress
Psychologists, 142
Psychology: study and teaching, 282,
288. *See also* College faculty
Psychotherapy, 106, 108, 244. *See
also* Counseling; Group
psychotherapy
Public officials, 266
Public spaces, 75
Public utilities, 167

Quid pro quo SH, 146, 264, 449,
464, 475

Rabidue v. Osceola Refining Co., 19
Race, 5, 75, 164, 169, 364, 407,
409, 412
Racism, 324, 407
Racketeer Influenced and Corrupt
Organizations Act (RICO), 489
Rape, 68, 83, 115, 121. *See also*
Assault
Rape Myth Acceptance Scale, 83
Reactance theory, 112

Reasonableness, 31, 80, 367, 419,
420, 422, 424, 425, 430, 432, 433,
434, 435, 440, 443, 447, 450, 454,
458, 459, 460, 462, 470, 474, 476,
477
Recovery, 489, 508
Redbook survey, 151
Reinstatement of harasser, 502, 514,
516
Religion, 32
Religion and perception of SH
behaviors, 79
Remedies, 497
Reporting of SH, 71, 111, 115, 232,
261, 283, 284, 330, 332, 340, 351
Reporting of SH and blame, 89
Reporting procedures. *See* Grievance
procedures
Reprisals, 156, 533
Research in SH: bibliographies, 13;
pathfinder, 429
Research issues, 1, 6, 9, 26, 28, 95,
331
Research recommendations, 4, 8
Researchers, 157
Residents (medical), 193, 203, 216
Response to SH. *See* Organizational
response; Victim response
Retroactivity, 488
*Ridge v. HCA Services of Kansas,
Inc.*, 178
Right to privacy. *See* Privacy, Right
to
*Robinson v. Jacksonville Shipyards,
Inc.*, 219, 230, 432, 455, 476, 480,
481, 484
Rokeach Value Survey, 63
Role playing, 174, 366
Role theory, 254, 350
Rosenberg Self-Esteem Scales, 71
Rotter Internet-External Locus of
Control Scale, 93
Rural population, 212

About the Authors

LYNDA JONES HARTEL is Instructor and Collection Development Librarian at the John A. Prior Health Sciences Library, The Ohio State University. She is an active member of the Special Libraries Association and numerous health sciences and academic library associations in Ohio. Her primary interests are in serial and consumer health collection development as well as women's issues.

HELENA M. VONVILLE is Internet Liaison Officer at AMIGOS Bibliographic Council, Inc. in Dallas, Texas. Previously, VonVille was a reference librarian at The Ohio State University in the Education/Psychology Library. Her publications have appeared in the journals *CD-ROM Librarian, Journal of Education for Library and Information Science,* and *Computers in Libraries,* as well as in the book *The Internet Library: Case Studies of Library Internet Management and Use.*

ISBN 0-313-29055-5

90000>

EAN

9 780313 290558

HARDCOVER BAR CODE